How Chandu Earned And Chinki Lost In The Stock Market?

By Mahesh Chander Kaushik

(NISM Certified Research Analyst Registered under SEBI RESEARCH ANALYSTS REGULATIONS, 2014, SEBI Registration Number INH 100000908)

"Chandu & Chinki are notional characters to understand my single stock trading formula practically. This story teaches that "How in 2005 they both invested INR 1-1 Lac in same stock (Arvind Mills) and Chinki lost his 236790 rupees but Chandu makes 242007 rupees. How is it possible? "

This book will change your whole strategy of investing in stock market.

PREFACE

Respected Readers,

Most of the small investors would be looking for a perfect trading system or " The Holy Grail For The Stock Market."

This book contains my secret trading system which is like the holy grail for me. This system would tell me exactly when to buy and when to sell stocks to make a maximum profit every time.

This book is my 2nd book on stock market investing. "The winning theory in stock market" is my first book where I told my basic concepts of stock market investing and now I write this book in fiction style, and I think this book is world's first stock market fiction.

If you are already familiar with my stock market blog www.maheshkaushik.com, then I think you also familiar with my notional characters of Chandu and Chinki.

Actually, I want to tell my secret sharegenius formula for trading cum long term investment.

After reading this book, you get replies of these questions:-

How to trading in a single stock?

or

How to accumulate a fancy stock? I develop this formula in 10 years of hard work and research on stock data.

So this book is written in fiction style where I told that how my notional character Chandu earn and Chinki loss from investment in same stock.

After reading this book:-

1. You may able to learn how to make huge profits in positional trade and make money through single stock trading.

2. You automatically understood when to buy or when to sell a stock.

" Yes, I invent a formula which automatically tells us that when we buy a stock and when we sell a stock. So after ten years hard work on stock data I invent this formula."

3. You may able to learn how to accumulate a large quantity of your fancy stock without any risk of money losing.

4. You may able to make money when a stock rise more and more and always quit early with a minimum loss when a stock starts big downfall.

5. You may able to learn how your portfolio will always be in profit.

I use the example of Arvind Limited to teaching this formula, but you can apply this formula to any stock.

This book contains my formula of fancy stock accumulating, and I told this formula in an interesting manner of chandu and chinki story.

I am sure that this book will change your mindset and you will surely make money through formula given in this book.

Regards

Mahesh Chander Kaushik
Assistant Revenue Accounts Officer
Collector Office. Dist. Sirohi
Rajasthan (India)
Email id: - mahesh2073@yahoo.com

My special thanks to:-

1. All of my blog followers, youtube channel followers, Sharegenius App followers and intelligent readers of my earlier book who give me the energy to write this book through his comments which showing continue faith and love on my theory.

2. Shri Shri 1008 Satynarayan Ji Falahari Baba, which is my guru (the spiritual teacher).

3. Respected Shri Maniram Setia retd. Principal which guides me in my childhood and makes my moral principles and teach me about work is worship.

-:Table of Contents:-

1

Chinki Dream About Arvind Mills Multibagger Story

It was the Friday night of 16 Sept 2005 when Chinki saw a dream that Arvind Mills stock touch the price of INR 415 and not only touch this high price stock of Arvind Mills demerger in two separate companies one name is Arvind Ltd the second name is Arvind Infrastructure Ltd.

In this dream, Chinki also saw that price of Arvind Infrastructure Ltd touch INR 95 which she gets after the demerger of Arvind Mills.

In her dream, she clearly saw that swap ratio between Arvind Ltd and Arvind Infrastructure is 10:1. This swap ratio means every ten shares of Arvind Ltd she gets 1 Share of Arvind infrastructure.Finally, her dream broken and she wakes up with a good hope.

When see awaken up from his sleep on 17 Sept 2005 Saturday morning she was very excited about her dream because Arvind Mills traded at 141 on 16 September 2005 (Friday). If she invested one lac rupees and bought 700 stocks of Arvind Ltd and things really happen as per her dream, then she will sell these 700 stocks @415 and earn a decent profit off 274 rupees per share.

It means she will earn INR 191800 rupees as profit and as per dream if she gets 70 extra shares of Arvind Infrastructure Ltd (In her dream she saw a swap ratio of 10:1 means if she bought 700 shares of Arvind Mills then she get 70 Share of Arvind Infra in future) so she multiply 70 X 95 (price of Arvind Infra which she saw in her dream)=6650 means she gets total profit of 191800 plus 6650 is equal to 198450, and she thinks this is not a bad idea to earn 198450 from an investment of 1,00,000.

The theoretical part of this story:- Small investors also saw these type of dreams when any broking house or analyst recommended target price of any stock, and due to faith on particular stock tip small investors also prepare their mindset to invest 1-2 lacs in single stocks to earn such decent profit.

So in this book, I tell you a formula that how to invest these 1-2 lacs in your fancy stock or any good stock to maximize return without fear of loss.

So keep reading this book because when you complete this book and follow my footprints, then no one can stop you to make huge returns from the stock market.

Why Chinki believes in her dreams:- When we sleep, we see dreams because seeing dreams during sleep is natural for humans. Generally, we ignore our dreams then why chinki so excited about her dreams?

Actually, from last few days Chinki practicing **"Tratka Gazing Meditation"** and after this meditation, she feels that her most of the dreams indicate incidents of future life.

(I suggest to readers that they search "Tratka Gazing Meditation for Future Indications" on google because if here I describe more details then it is out of subject of this book)

So after this dream, she thinks that her subconscious mind indicates the future price of this stock, so she has a good chance to get decent profits.

It happens 2-3 times when she saw future price of stocks in dreams and that price would come in stock market, so this time she has blind faith in this dream

When investor got 2-3 right calls from any analyst, then they also develop a blind faith of these calls, and they invest huge money in the 4th call. If unfortunately after 3 best calls 4th call will underperform then all of their money will trap in a single stock. Sometimes my followers also face this situation, so I write this book to teach that how to invest a huge amount in single stock which you believe as future multi-bagger stock.

So Chinki decided to invest her 1 lac rupees in Arvind mills when market open on 19 Sept 2005 (Monday).

2

Chandu And Chinki Meeting With Me

On 18 September 2015 Chinki meet with his best friend, Chandu.

" Hi, Chinki why your face is so glowing? Chandu asked.

" Chandu I am so happy because I find an idea to earn near 2 Lac rupees from stock market" Chinki replied.

" Oh, Really? Chandu asked.

" Yes, I saw a dream of the stock tip," Chinki replied.

Chandu laughed near 1 minute and said: " Chinki you are such innocent, I think dreams are dreams so forget it and enjoy our ice-cream cones which I just ordered for you."

"No Chandu, I cannot forget it because due to my practice of tratka meditation my last 3 dreams become true for example before 2 months I saw a dream that you laugh on my dreams, and I wonder to see that this dream just now changes in reality, so it increases my overall faith

So I am going to invest my whole saving of INR 1 lac in Arvind Mills on Monday" Chinki Announced.

"OK, my dear but I think we both consult with Mahesh Kaushik I follow his sharegenius blog and I think before investing your whole saving his advice may protect your money," Chandu say.

" I am not interested in his advice because I knew he never advises to put all savings in single stock, but it is interesting to know that what formula he suggest to invest my 1 lac in Arvind Mills So I am ready to consult with him,"Chinki replied.

Chandu asks an appointment with me, and fortunately, it was a Sunday, so I am free with my government job, so I give an immediate appointment to Chandu and Chinki.

 They come at my home and tell me about Chinki dream and her wish to invest all of his savings in Arvind Mills.

I Check Arvind Ltd year 2004-05 net sale which was 1678.86 Cr., and the total number of equity shares was 23,00,00,000 So net sale per share of 2004-05 was 72.99 and stock already traded at 141 so due to Arvind Mills low net sale per share for 2004-05 I advised them that forget to buy it now and if stock available below 72 then Arvind Mills is a good buy.

(If you are a new reader and not familiar with my net sale per share concept then I advise you to read my earlier book "The Winning Theory in Stock Market.)

Chinki refused my advice and announced " I am not going to change my decision to invest 1 lac rupees in Arvind Mills share.

She argued " Many stocks of Indian stock market traded many times higher than their net sale per share, so It is possible that Arvind Ltd also touches 415 in future.

I replied " Chinki I do not challenge the power of your subconscious mind which tell you a future price and future demerger of Arvind Mills but your dreams not describe a time period that how many time they take to convert in reality suppose this indication show after 10-15 year future price then why you trap your money now?

Chandu was laughing during my reply ; Chinki takes it as her insult, so she warns Chandu " Chandu if you really love me then you also invest your 1 lac in this stock.

Now Chandu falls in religious crises because in one side his love wishes that he also invest a huge amount in her suggested stock and in the second side my advice that not to invest at this level.

Chandu was a strict follower of me and never ignore my advice, so Chandu feels trapped in religious crises between his love(Chinki) and his faith in me.

So he prayer to me " Guru ji what to do now?

OK, Do not worry, Chinki I have a solution. I invent a formula about investing a huge amount in a fancy stock, so I told this secret trading cum investing formula to both of you.

If you like this, then you and Chandu both invest there 1-1 lacs rupees in Arvind Mills through this safe manner which I tell you.

At this movement, my wife comes with tea and snacks, and after our tea break, I start exploring my idea.

3

My Secret Formula For Investment Cum Trading In Any Single Stock.

When we finish our tea and snacks, I start telling my simple investment cum trading formula which work in any market condition and on any regularly traded stock.

Outline of Sharegenius Investment Formula:-

1.Choose your fancy stock or any stock which is coming multi-bagger in your view or any analyst view .

2. Download last 1-year price data of your chosen stock from stock exchange website in MS Excel format.

Chandu stopped me here and asked " One minute sir, I do not know how to download price data from exchange website?

I replied, " OK, do not worry Chandu, when we complete this outline then I tell you a method that how you download price data from stock exchange website."

3. Delete open price, high price, low price, columns in your Excel sheet which you

download from BSE site. We need only date and closer price column.

4. Calculate "200DMA" in a column.

If you do not know how to calculate 200 DMA, then do not worry because, in next pages of this book, I am also told full method of 200DMA calculations.

5. In next column calculate the difference between close price and 200DMA (Close Price -200DMA).

6. Finally, calculate the difference between close price and 200 DMA in percentage (%) terms.

Do not worry I tell everything that how to calculate point 3 to 6, here I only give an outline, but in next pages, I tell complete method practically so, please keep reading this book until the last page.

Please do not Skip any page of this book and read it page by page even somewhere you feel boring but do not skip any page because if you read all page of this book, you get a new world of safe investment.

Now your "sharegenius software for trading cum investment in stocks" is ready.

7. Divide your decided investment amount into 20 parts.

For example, If you decided to invest 1 lac then divide it 20 parts of 5000-5000 each or If you decide to invest 2 lac then divide it 20 parts of 10,000-10,000 each.

If you want to invest only INR 50,000, then divide it 20 parts of 2500-2500 each.

8. Now Check your software in MS Excel sheet, if your stock traded below his 200 DMA then this is not a right time to invest in this stock just hold your money in cash and earn saving account interest on your cash during the time period until your stock crosses his 200 DMA in the upside.

9. If your stock traded above his 200 DMA, then check how many percentages it up from closing price?

10. I hope you remember table of five , 5,10,15,20,25,30,35,40,45,50,55,60,65,70…..and so on.

11. For every 5% rise from 200 DMA we invest our 1 part of money, We divide our money in 20 part of 5000-5000 each so if Chinki dream really become true we invest our 5000 when stock rises 5% up from 200 DMA, when stock rises 10% from 200DMA we put our next 5000 in this

stock, when stock rises 15% from 200 DMA we put our next 3rd part of 5000 in this stock.

12. *Suppose your stock last closed price 16% up from 200 DMA, then for first-time entry in game wait until next five multiple level comes on the closing basis.*

It means for first time entry in that stock you wait until stock close 20% above from 200 DMA because next five multiple after 16 is 20 .

If you make an Excel sheet and find your stock traded 5.65% above 200 DMA then as per this rule, for first time entry in this stock you will wait until stock close above next five multiple levels , it is 10% in case of 5.65% (**If you do not understand this point clearly then do not worry I explain everything in next pages, please keep patience.**)

13. For every 5% downfall from 200 DMA, we sell our one lot (one part).

If the stock falls 10% from 200 DMA, then we sell another part.

If the stock falls 15% from 200 DMA, then we sell our 3rd part as first come first serve policy we sell our oldest buying first.

So every 5% fall from 200 DMA we sell one part of our holding and every 5% rise from 200 DMA we invest one part of our money.

And Chinki If your dream is really true then as Arvind Mills (Arvind Ltd is formally known as Arvind Mills) rise our investment is also rising and if your dream is the only dream, and price will fall as my net sale per share theory then this formula protect our investment, and we sell our stocks as price will fall.

Chinki Said " Sir, I am so excited to make more money, and if I follow your formula, then it will limit my profits. So sorry sir I am not going to follow you, but If Chandu wants to follow your theory, then I have no problem.

Chandu was very happy now and said " Thank you Chinki and Mahesh Sir, I definitely follow this sharegenius holy grail. I believe this perfect trading system will win over Chinki one time investment.

They both thanks to me for my time and returned to their homes.

4

Practically Implement of Sharegenius Investment Formula On Arvind Ltd Stock.

On 19 September 2005 when Indian stock market open Chinki invest her entire saving 1,00,000 in Arvind Mills Stock.

Arvind Ltd (BSE Code 500101) was formerly known as Arvind Mills.

Kindly download historical price data of Arvind Ltd from 1 September 2004 to 31 Oct 2016 from this link:-

http://www.bseindia.com/markets/equity/EQRep orts/StockPrcHistori.aspx?expandable=7&scripc ode=500101&flag=sp&Submit=G

These historical prices are required for a more deep understanding of this book.

If you feel difficulties to download historical price, then please read my blog post from this link:-

http://sharegenius.maheshkaushik.com/2015/07/how-to-find-historical-stock-price-of.html

So on 19 Sept 2005 price of Arvind Ltd was 140 to 143.90 and Chinki buy 710 Shares at price of 140.85

Total investment=140.85*710=1,00,003.50 (Near one lac rupees).

On the other side, Chandu makes an MS Excel sheet as per my formula.

First of all Chandu download historical price of Arvind Ltd from 1 Sept 2004 to 19 Sept 2005.

I already tell you about " how to download historical price data of any stock from BSE site?".

After download MS Excel sheet Chandu deletes open price, high price, low price, columns.

Chandu needs only date and closer price column.

Now he calculates 200 DMA in one column, variation from close price-200 DMA in another column and % Variation in the 3rd column.

I knew some of the readers still feel difficulties to understand clearly, so I provide you this complete MS Excel sheet on my google drive download it from here:-

https://drive.google.com/file/d/0BwqVx444SxLa anRPMzJXamJ4UmM/view?usp=sharing

Or watch my youtube video about 200 DMA calculation method:-

https://www.youtube.com/watch?v=rSVbuSddV BU

Now data of Chandu MS Excel sheet looks like this picture:-

Chandu MS Excel Sheet of Sharegenius Software with Arvind Ltd				
Date	Close Price	200 DMA	Change	% Variation
1-Sep-04	81.35	In first 200 row you cannot find 200		
2-Sep-04	81.85	DMA because for calculating 200 DMA		
3-Sep-04	82.8	we need 200 Days closing price so in		
6-Sep-04	82.9	row 202 we put a formula =Sum		
7-Sep-04	82.2	(B3:B202)/200 means sum of B3 to B202		
8-Sep-04	82.25	closing price divide by 200 to getting		
9-Sep-04	81.15	200 DMA here formula start from B3		
10-Sep-04	80.8	because B1 and B2 are headings		
13-Sep-04	82			
14-Sep-04	79.7			
15-Sep-04	80.35			
16-Sep-04	80.5			
17-Sep-04	80.2			

So as on 19 Sept 2005, Chandu see Arvind Mill 200 DMA was 126.24, and the stock closed at

141.25 which is 10.63% above from his 200 DMA.

See Chandu Excel sheet data on 19 Sept 2005 in this picture:-

Chandu MS Excel Sheet of Sharegenius Software with Arvind Ltd

Date	Close Price	200 DMA	Change	% Variation
6-Sep-05	133.4	125.17	8.23	6.17
8-Sep-05	136.25	125.36	10.89	8.00
9-Sep-05	136.25	125.49	10.76	7.89
12-Sep-05	137.45	125.62	11.83	8.60
13-Sep-05	139.85	125.74	14.11	10.09
14-Sep-05	135.6	125.85	9.75	7.19
15-Sep-05	137.05	125.97	11.08	8.09
16-Sep-05	141	126.10	14.90	10.57
19-Sep-05	141.25	126.24	15.01	10.63
20-Sep-05	139.6	126.36	13.24	9.48

When Chandu watch this 10.63 % Variation from 200 DMA ,Chandu think as per my formula stock cross two level of 5% and 10% so he should invest his 2 part of the money (Two part of money means he should invest his INR5000*2=INR 10,000 at this level.)

Because he remember that I said " If your stock close above his 200DMA then check how many % is traded up from his 200 DMA and every multiple of 5 you invest your one part of money, So when he find stock traded 10.63% above 200 DMA then he think it means he invest 2 parts of his money one for 5% upside and Second for 10% upside.

He also put this sheet for my observation and confirmation.

After viewing his sheet, I smiled and said: " Chandu you forget to implement point 12 of my rule in your sheet because I said at this point that *"For first-time entry in the game wait until next five multiple levels come on closing basis."*

Now Arvind Mills is 10.63% up from 200 DMA, so we cannot invest until Arvind stock close above next five multiple levels which is 15%.

So do not invest at this level because your 19 Sept 2005 closing price show 10.63% upside from 200 DMA and you want to take your first-time entry in the game so wait until Arvind stock close above 15% from 200 DMA.

For example, if stock close 15% above from his 200 DMA then we start our investment with one part of our money and invest other parts on 20%,25%,30%,35%,40%,45%.....rising from 200 DMA.

So As on 19 Sept 2005 Chinki Buy 710 Shares of Arvind Ltd and invest near 1 lac Indian rupees, but Chandu did not buy any share because he waits for a right time when stock close 15% above from his 200 DMA and he hold all cash 1,00,000 rupees in his saving account.

5

What Happen During 19 Sept 2005 to 19 Sept 2006

Now Chinki holds 710 Shares of Arvind Ltd and Chandu hold cash of 1 lac Indian rupees.

Chandu opened his excel sheet per day and enter the closing price, after entering closing price his sheet formulas calculate 200 DMA and % variation from 200 DMA and this whole process took his 5 minutes per day.

If you download this sheet from the link provided in the earlier chapter, then you may see that after 19 Sept 2005 stock not closed 15 % above from his 200 DMA.

From 14 Oct 2005 Arvind Ltd start falling below his 200 DMA, Here Chandu not hold any stock , If he holds at these levels then he may sell one lot at every 5% fall, but here his holding was Nil so he cannot sell any share I give this example only for your easy reference.

Date	Close Price	200 DMA	Change	% Variation
Chandu MS Excel Sheet of Sharegenius Software with Arvind Ltd				
13-Oct-05	132.25	127.74	4.51	3.41
14-Oct-05	126.15	127.71	-1.56	-1.23
17-Oct-05	122.5	127.69	-5.19	-4.23
18-Oct-05	122.35	127.64	-5.29	-4.32
19-Oct-05	120.35	127.57	-7.22	-6.00
20-Oct-05	113.5	127.47	-13.97	-12.31
21-Oct-05	119.45	127.45	-8.00	-6.70

If Chandu hold any shares on 19 Oct 2005 when Arvind close 6% below from 200 DMA then on next day 20 Oct 2005 he may sell his oldest buying as first come first serve theory, Same happen on 20 Oct 2005 when stock fall 12.31% below from 200 DMA in this situation Chandu may sell his 2nd oldest buying on next trading day of 21 Oct 2005, However here Chandu have no any stock for sale.

If you do not download complete excel sheet which I provided on my google drive, then I again request you that please download complete sheet and take a print and refer this sheet as you continue with this book.

Link for Download:-

https://drive.google.com/file/d/0BwqVx444SxLa anRPMzJXamJ4UmM/view?usp=sharing

So if you refer your sheet and go to 19 Sept 2006 date then what you find?

During this one year Arvind never close above his 200 DMA so Chandu still on cash and get a 4% saving account interest INR 4000 on his saving account Now his net worth is 1,04,000 but what happen with Chinki?

See these price data of 19 Sept 2006 for calculating Chinki net worth:-

Chandu MS Excel Sheet of Sharegenius Software with Arvind Ltd

Date	Close Price	200 DMA	Change	% Variation
19-Sep-06	66.85	82.44	-15.59	-23.33
20-Sep-06	65.85	82.23	-16.38	-24.87

So if we multiply 19 Sept 2006 Closing price 66.85 with 710 shares, then it is 710 x 66.85=47463.50.

Oh, Chinki lost his 52540 rupees?

On 19 Sept Chandu and Chinki meet in a cafe and during, they enjoyed his Cofee Chandu smile and asked "Chinki now you agree that Mahesh Kaushik is right? Because you almost lost your 52540 rupees, but I earn a saving account interest of INR 4000.

Now Chinki lose her temper again and say " I watch a video of your foolish Mahesh Kaushik where he says do not worry from your notional loss just hold your stocks and wait for a good time?"

She took a sip of hot coffee and continued her hot talk "So why you call my notional loss as a permanent loss, I still hold my 710 shares, and I am a long term investor one day I get a decent profit from this company."

"Chandu you have a good chance if you forget your teacher advice and buy at this level 66.85 then you have more chance to get profit soon." She advised.

" No Chinki, I am a strict follower of Mahesh Kaushik, and I enjoy my peaceful mind due to his software. Chandu replied.

Finally, Chinki said "Ok dear, Next year we both meet again and compare our portfolio if you still won then I give you a party, and if you did not win after 1 year you give me a party.

Chandu laughed and accepted her challenge and pay the coffee bill.

6

What Happen During 19 Sept 2006 to 19 Sept 2007

During 19 Sept 2006 to 31 Aug 2007 Arvind stock continue traded below his 200 DMA, I think you already download complete Excel sheet and watch data from 19 Sept 2006 to 31 Aug 2007, If you do not download complete sheet yet then refer this picture:-

Chandu MS Excel Sheet of Sharegenius Software with Arvind Ltd

Date	Close Price	200 DMA	Change	% Variation
30-Aug-07	46.35	48.54	-2.19	-4.71
31-Aug-07	48	48.49	-0.49	-1.03
3-Sep-07	51.5	48.47	3.03	5.89
4-Sep-07	52.4	48.45	3.95	7.53
5-Sep-07	51.9	48.44	3.46	6.66

But one day on 3-Sep-07 a magic happen with Arvind Ltd stock and the stock closed at 51.50 which is 5.89% above from his 200 DMA 48.47.

Chandu thinks now he waits from 15 % above close for fresh buy but at 8.00 PM of 3-Sep-07, Chandu received a phone call from me.

I say " Hello Chandu is there?"

Chandu replied, "Oh sir what a pleasant surprise that you call me."

" Chandu, when you and Chinki meet with me on 18 Sept 2005 I am not told an important part of my formula to you because if that time I told this part to you then you do not understand it clearly."

"Oh sir, please tell me what thing you hide from me?"

"Not hide my dear, that time is not a right time to clarify full formula because if I continue that time without any practical example, then you may feel boring and not understand clearly."

"Ok, sir,Please tell me remaining part of your sharegenius rule."Chandu was excited.

I replied:-

" *Whenever your stock % variation from 200 DMA recover from (-) sign to (+) sign then every time you consider it as a starting point . it means if your stock recovers from (-)% variation below 200 DMA to (+)% variation above 200 DMA then you buy your one lot (start investing with one part of your money).* "

Because recovering from below 200 DMA to above 200 DMA is a strong technical signal you do not need to learn full technical analysis you only consider (+) and (-) variation from 200 DMA so now see today condition of Arvind:-

Chandu MS Excel Sheet of Sharegenius Software with Arvind Ltd

Date	Close Price	200 DMA	Change	% Variation
30-Aug-07	46.35	48.54	-2.19	-4.71
31-Aug-07	48	48.49	-0.49	-1.03
3-Sep-07	51.5	48.47	3.03	5.89
4-Sep-07	52.4	48.45	3.95	7.53
5-Sep-07	51.9	48.44	3.46	6.66

You see that stock close at 51.50 which is 5.89% higher from 200 DMA so you may start your investing from here and invest your 1/20 part of money means if you decided to invest total 1,00,000 in Arvind then invest your first 5000 at this level."

Chandu Argued " But sir you say I wait till 15% above from 200 DMA."

"Yes, my dear but do not forget my rule that Whenever your stock % variation from 200 DMA recover from (-) sign to (+) sign then every time you consider it as a starting point ." I replied.

"OK, sir now I understand that on 3 Sept 2007 Arvind price % variation shift from -1.03% to +5.89% so I can start from here and in future whenever this situation happens I consider it as a fresh starting level."

" Yes, same happen in downside that Whenever your stock % variation from 200 DMA down from (+) sign to (-) sign then every time you consider it as a fresh selling point".

Chandu understand my point, and he want to put a buy order for Arvind Ltd at 3 Sept 2007 closing price of 51.50 but I also advised him that **whenever you put an off market buy order then always put 1 % upper price in limit price because if any stock technically sound then it may be possible a gap up opening in next trading session, and if next day stock open above 51.50 and 51.50 not come during market time then you lost your buying opportunity.**

So do not put off-market buying order @51.50 per share instead of this put 1% upper price means 1% of 51.50 is 0.5150 so put your limit price 51.50+0.51=52.01 that will be sure you buy your stock in next trading session.

If next day stock opens below 52.01, then exchange automatic made your trade at a lower price so do not worry about it.

So Chandu put his off-market buying order @52.01 per share and ordered to buy 96 shares for next trading session of 04 Sep 2007.

Chandu bought total 96 shares and invests INR 4992.96 (For easy calculation I ignore brokerage amount in these examples) Chandu holds remaining cash 104000-4992.96= INR 99007.04.

On 13 Sept 2007 Arvind stock closed at 54 rupees, so this was 10.22% up from that day 200 DMA, See in this picture:-

Chandu MS Excel Sheet of Sharegenius Software with Arvind Ltd

Date	Close Price	200 DMA	Change	% Variation
6-Sep-07	52.25	48.44	3.81	7.29
7-Sep-07	50.95	48.44	2.51	4.93
10-Sep-07	52	48.45	3.55	6.82
11-Sep-07	52.55	48.46	4.09	7.78
12-Sep-07	51.4	48.46	2.94	5.72
13-Sep-07	54	48.48	5.52	10.22

So as per my rule, he put an off-market order on 13 Sept 2007 night; Chandu added 1% of 54 = 0.54 in his off-market order for preventing gap up opening. Chandu ordered to buy 92 shares @

54+0.54=54.54 when the market opens on 14 Sept 2007.

Chandu bought 92 more shares on 14 Sept 2007 @ 54.54 and invested INR 5017.68 (Without brokerage, I already tell that we ignore brokerage for easy calculation.) So now his remaining cash is 99007.04-5017.68=93989.36, and he holds 96+92=188 shares of Arvind Mills.

On 19 Sept 2007 Chandu and Chinki again meet in a hotel and discuss their portfolio, Chinki situation was:-

Chinki holds 710 shares and market value of her investment was 710x50.60= 35926, and she faces a notional loss of INR 64074.

Chandu hold 188 shares and market value of his 188 shares was 188x50.60=9512.80

Chandu saving account balance since last 11 months was 1,04,000, and in 12 months he invests INR 10120 from this balance, so he also gets 4% saving account interest of 4020 for this year.

Chandu total cash=93880+4020=97900.

Chandu net worth= 97900 Cash + 9512.80 Equity=107412.80.

So who was won?

Of course, Chandu is won. As per Chinki promise of earlier year, Chinki wanted to give an ice cream party, but Chandu waved off his party and said " Chinki you are already at a loss, so I will pay the bill of our ice cream party. I think now you use Mahesh Kaushik " Loss Recovery Idea" to recover your loss.

Chinki wondered " What is this idea Chandu?

Chandu said " In his book The Winning Theory of Stock Market he told this idea in Chapter 26 page 97 of his book he said **When your stock cross this 200 DMA from lower price to higher price and you still hold that stock in loss then average out at this level and invest the double amount in that stock.**"

Chandu take a breath and continue

" You already invest 1 lac and hold 710 shares of Arvind Mills, and now stock cross his 200 DMA from downside to upside so as per this idea you require to invest 2 lac at this level of 50.60 and if you average out from this method then you may buy 3953 more shares at 50.60 level this will reduce your cost of holding to 64.33 rupees per share (300000/4663=64.33) So as per Mahesh Kaushik in 80% cases this price 64.33 will come within 1-2 months, and you recover your whole loss from this method."

Chinki agreed with Chandu and ordered my book " **The Winning Theory in Stock Market**" for more detail of my loss recover idea.

7

Chinki Average Out Arvind

On 20 Sept 2007 Chinki want to average out his loss-making holding so as per Chandu advice she uses my smart average out method and invest 2 lac fresh money at the level of 50.60.

Chinki buy 3953 more shares at the rate of 50.60

So after this average out Chinki hold 3953+710=4663 shares of Arvind Ltd so after this average out her cost of holding reduced to INR 64.33 rupees per share (300000/4663=64.33).

See 4 Oct 2007 closing price in your Excel sheet which you already download before start reading this story of if you do not download this sheet then see this picture:-

Chandu MS Excel Sheet of Sharegenius Software with Arvind Ltd

Date	Close Price	200 DMA	Change	% Variation
26-Sep-07	59.75	48.45	11.30	18.91
27-Sep-07	58.2	48.47	9.73	16.72
28-Sep-07	61.9	48.51	13.39	21.63
1-Oct-07	63	48.57	14.43	22.90
3-Oct-07	61.5	48.64	12.86	20.91
4-Oct-07	65.3	48.71	16.59	25.40

Chinki wondered that within 15 days of her

average out stock closed @65.30 on 04 Oct 2007 so at this rate, she recovers her full loss and sits on profit because now market value of her portfolio was 4663x65.30=304493.90 So If she sells stock here then she gets 4493.90 as profit.

Chandu calls him " Hello Chinki, Congratulations now I think you sell your stocks at 65.30 and get rid of your losses. I think now you understand what Mahesh Kaushik want to say?"

Chinki replied, " Yes Chandu now I am also a disciple of Mahesh Kaushik, but before I book my profit I want to ask one thing to you that how many Arvind stocks you hold today?"

Chandu replied " Chinki you knew that on 19 Sept 2007 I hold 188 shares of Arvind but as stock price goes up my software automatic trigger fresh buying suggestion and I buy 163 more shares at 15% and 20% upside from 200 DMA, and now I hold total 351 stocks plus my software trigger that today stock closed 25.40% above from 200 DMA, so I am going to buy 76 more shares on next trading session."

Before we continue I want to explain about Chandu buying, See your excel sheet which you download on starting of this book or refer this picture:-

Chandu MS Excel Sheet of Sharegenius Software with Arvind Ltd

Date	Close Price	200 DMA	Change	% Variation
26-Sep-07	59.75	48.45	11.30	18.91
27-Sep-07	58.2	48.47	9.73	16.72
28-Sep-07	61.9	48.51	13.39	21.63
1-Oct-07	63	48.57	14.43	22.90
3-Oct-07	61.5	48.64	12.86	20.91
4-Oct-07	65.3	48.71	16.59	25.40

On 26 Sept 2007, Arvind closed 18.91% above from his 200 DMA; Chandu already bought for 5% and 10% upside, so this was the time for 15% upside buy.

The stock closed 18.91% above from 200 DMA, so Chandu ordered his next lot for 15%, It means he fill buying price 59.75+0.59=60.34 and buy 83 more shares by the investment of 5008.22, Now total share 188+83=271 and remaining cash was 93001.14.

On 28 Sept 2007

Closed price 61.90

21.63 % above from 200 DMA

Time to order for 20%+ upside

Ordered 80 more share @62.51 (61.90+0.61)

Fresh investment=80x62.51=5000.80

Total share on 29 Sept 2007= 271+80=351

Remain Cash = 93001.14-5000.80=88000.34

For easy calculation, I ignore Brokerage on these examples.

On 4 Oct 2007

Closed price 65.30

25.40 % above from 200 DMA

Time to order for 25%+ upside

Ordered 76 more share @65.95 (65.30+0.65)

Fresh investment=76x65.95=5012.20

Remain Cash = 88000.34-5012.20=82988.14

Total share on 05 Oct 2007= 351+76=427

For easy calculation, I ignore Brokerage on these examples.

Now we again come to our story.

After hearing Chandu reply, Chinki argued " Chandu are you mad? You going to buy 76 more shares and advised me to sell out my stocks? Do you think this is logical? I think this stock is now starting his upward journey and my dream will become true that one day Arvind Mills stocks touch the price of INR 415 and not only touch this high price stock of Arvind Mills demerger in two separate companies one name is Arvind Ltd the second name is Arvind infrastructure Ltd.

So I continue to hold it because I am a long term investor for 10-20 years and not sell my stocks till 10-20 years.

Chandu replied " But Chinki you want to recover your loss, and now you recovered it then why you change your mind?

" I Changed my mind because you still want to buy this stock and when your software tells you a suggestion for sell, then I am also selling my stocks."

"Oh my dear, my software triggered for sell when Arvind close -5% below from his 200 DMA that time you again trap in the loss, and you do not sell it that time in the loss."

" No Chandu, If you do not worry from a loss, then I think it is not wise to sell my holdings."

So Chinki mixes her greed in my "loss recover idea" and continue to hold her stocks instead of recovering his loss.

8

What Happens in 2008 Largest Stock Market Crash.

I am an honest person, so I start this story from 19 Sept 2005 because I want to tell you worse situation with my formula because in 2008 Indian and the international stock market was crashed and face largest stock market fall in world history.

So in this chapter, I tell you that if you hold a stock as per my software, then "what worst situation you may face in the stock market crash?".

Now we continue with Chandu software see you excel sheet or this picture:-

Chandu MS Excel Sheet of Sharegenius Software with Arvind Ltd

Date	Close Price	200 DMA	Change	% Variation
15-Oct-07	72.7	49.20	23.50	32.32
16-Oct-07	70.35	49.30	21.05	29.93
17-Oct-07	67.15	49.37	17.78	26.48
18-Oct-07	66.85	49.44	17.41	26.04

On 15 Oct 2007

Closed price 72.70

32.32 % above from 200 DMA

Time to order for 30%+ upside

Ordered 69 more share @73.42 (72.70+0.72)

Fresh investment=69x73.42=5065.98

Remain Cash = 82988.14-5065.98=77922.16

Total share on 16 Oct 2007= 427+69=496

For easy calculation, I ignore Brokerage on these examples.

Chandu MS Excel Sheet of Sharegenius Software with Arvind Ltd				
Date	Close Price	200 DMA	Change	% Variation
4-Dec-07	80.9	52.04	28.86	35.67
5-Dec-07	79.55	52.17	27.38	34.42
6-Dec-07	76.8	52.29	24.51	31.92

On 04 Dec 2007

Closed price 80.90

35.67 % above from 200 DMA

Time to order for 35%+ upside

Ordered 61 more shares @81.70 (80.90+0.80)

Fresh investment=61x81.70=4983.70

Remain Cash = 77922.16-4983.70=72938.46

Total share on 05 Dec 2007= 496+61=557

For easy calculation, I ignore Brokerage on these examples.

On 31 Dec 2007, Chandu and Chinki meet in a new year party "Welcome 2008" where they both discuss their portfolio again.

Now Closing price of Arvind was 90.55

Chinki hold 4663 shares and market value of her shares was 4663x90.55=422234.65, So Chinki sit on 122234.65 net profit, and Chandu hold 557 Stocks market value of his stocks was 557x90.55=50436.35

Chandu also holds 72938.46 rupees in Cash.

Chandu net worth was 50436.35 + 72938.46 = 123374.81

They both were happy and enjoyed their new year party; Chandu again asks to Chinki " Chinki suppose Arvind Mills down again near 50 and your portfolio again convert in the loss , in this situation you book loss or wait more time?

Chinki replied " Chandu you hear about Warren Buffett?

Chandu said, " yes, I knew he is a big investor in the USA."

Chinki asked, " are you knew about his investment strategy?"

Chandu said, " No,but I will be happy if you put some light on warren buffet investment strategy."

Then Chinki tells him a story.

At 11 years old, Buffett bought his first stock – 6 shares of Cities Service (now known as CITGO – an Oil company) at $38 per share. He bought 3 for himself and 3 for his sister Doris.

That is all the money he had at that time. Practiced little to no diversification at a young age which he continued to do throughout his investment career.

The stock price fell to $27 but soon went to $40. He sold the stock at $40, but, the stock shot up to $202 in the next few years.

He later cited this experience as an early lesson in patience in investing.

So Chandu I am a follower of Warren Buffet and never sell my stocks in the loss.

Chandu was silent and enjoy her drink.

On 21 Jan 2008

Indian and International stock markets crash badly and Arvind stock down from 71.10 to 53.95.

See your excel sheet or this picture:-

Chandu MS Excel Sheet of Sharegenius Software with Arvind Ltd

Date	Close Price	200 DMA	Change	% Variation
17-Jan-08	76.3	57.26	19.04	24.95
18-Jan-08	71.1	57.41	13.69	19.26
21-Jan-08	53.95	57.46	-3.51	-6.51
22-Jan-08	41.75	57.45	-15.70	-37.61
23-Jan-08	48.55	57.46	-8.91	-18.36

So as on 21 Jan 2008 Arvind Stock close -6.51% below from 200 DMA. Stock close more than -5% below from 200 DMA this is the sign of start selling.

As first come first serve rule Chandu want to sell his first lot of 96 shares which Chandu buy on 04 Sept 2007 @52.01.

 So Chandu fill a sell order for 96 shares 1% below from 21 Jan 2008, **As per my rule when we want to put an off-market buying order then we fill 1% upper price and if we want to put a sell order then we need to fill 1% lower**

price for preventing gap up or gap down opening.

So here Chandu fill 53.95-0.53=53.42 limit price for sell his 96 shares on next trading session of 22 Jan 2008.

I tell earlier that 2008 stock market fall is world largest fall. So on 22 Jan 2008 Arvind stock open at 49 and touch a high of 52.50.

Chandu limit price 53.42 did not come on 22 Jan 2008; **This is the reason why I say you feed a price 1% lower from the closing price when you want to sell on next day**.

Due to 2008 largest stock market fall, this was an exceptional case otherwise 1% lower or 1% higher price is sufficient for executing an off-market limit order on next trading session.

On 22 Jan 2008 Arvind stock closed on 41.75 which is -37.61% below from 200 DMA, so this was a sign of selling 7 lots at once one for -5% Second for -10%, third for -15% and so on and finally 7th lot for -35% fall.

In a normal market, **you never find this type of situation when my sharegenius software triggers 7 lot in a single day, but 2008 fall is a**

big fall where stock price down 71 to 41 within 2 days.

So Chandu feeds an off-market order @41.34 (1% below from 22 Jan closed price 41.75)sell all of his 7 lots as below picture:-

Chandu Balance Sheet from 19 Sept 2005				
Date	Buy	Price @	Total Inestment	Cash in hand
5-Sep-07	96	52.01	4992.96	99007.04
14-Sep-07	92	54.54	5017.68	93989.36
27-Sep-07	83	60.34	5008.22	93001.14
1-Oct-07	80	62.51	5000.8	88000.34
5-Oct-07	76	65.95	5012.2	82988.14
16-Oct-07	69	73.42	5065.98	77922.16
5-Dec-07	61	81.7	4983.7	72938.46
total	557		35081.54	
Date	sell	Price @	Total Amount get	
23-Jan-08	557	46	25622	98560.46
Net Loss			9459.54	

Here you see selling price was 46 instead of 41.34 because on the night of 22 Jan 2008 Chandu put his sell order for a limit price of 41.34 but next trading day on 23 Jan 2008 Arvind stock open @46 so exchange automatic sell stock at an open price of 46.

So Chandu sells all of his 557 stocks and books a net loss of 9459.54.

I want to clarify to my readers that they do not be disappointed.

Because 2008 stock market fall is a world largest stock market crash. So, from this example, I want to teach you that what worst situation you may face if you follow my method.

This loss of INR 9459.54 is actually not a loss because if you read my earlier book " The Winning Theory in Stock Market" and familiar with my "Reverse Trading System" theory then you knew this type of selling is known as "Reverse Trading System" where we buy our sold stock again at a lower price.

So with this system you always sit on cash when your stock is down but when your stock is rise you hold and increase your holding as stock rise.

For example, If Chandu sells his 557 stocks on 31 Dec 2007 when the price of this stock is 90.55 then he got a profit of INR 23374.81, but here I not told a trading method I want to tell method of buying for long term 10+ years holding.

OK, now we continue our story and see what happen with Chinki stocks.

Chinki hold 4663 shares and after this market fall at 23 Jan 2008 closing price @48.55 market value of Chinki stocks was 48.55x4663=226388.65, and you remember 31 Dec 2007 market value of these stocks were 422234.65, So this market fall forfeit all of Chinki profit INR 122234.65 and turn around his portfolio from profit to loss of INR-73611.35.

Chandu called the Chinki " Hellow Chinki are you fine?

Chinki replied " What happen Chandu , I am absolutely fine, why you ask this question?

"Chinki you lost near 2 lac (1.22 lac notional profit and 0.73 lac principle amount) in the stock market, so I am worried about you," Chandu said.

" Oh, Chandu forget about my investment because I am a long term investor like Warren Buffett but what happen with your investment?"

"Chinki today I sell all of my 557 shares @46 and book my loss of INR 9459.54 because Mahesh Kaushik software show a sell sign for all of my 7 lots and I think this is a sign of big downtrend and stock will not trigger revival again in near future, so I got a chance of buy again at lower price."

"Ha, Ha, Ha" Chinki laughed.

"Why you laughed Chinki," Chandu asked

" I think one day your foolish guru has drowned you in big losses because today Arvind stock is revival again and closed @48.55 which is 2.55 rupees higher from your selling price of 46 rupees so If you follow him, then you book such type of loss every time," Chinki replied.

" No Chinki, I do not think so, I think you may also sell your 4663 shares and book your loss as Mahesh Kaushik reverse trading system because you may get a chance of buying again at a lower price from here," Chandu advised.

"Not at all Chandu , I am not a foolish like your guru, I am a long term investor like Warren Buffett and hold my stock for the 10-year view, so I am not worried if my stock further falls from here," Chinki replied.

"OK, Chinki good night."

"Good night dear and best of luck," Chinki said.

9

3 Year Return of Chandu and Chinki

On 19 Sept 2008, Chandu and Chinki again meet in a hotel, and Chandu ordered 2 ice cream cone.

Here we see 19 Sept 2008 situation of Arvind stock:-

Chandu MS Excel Sheet of Sharegenius Software with Arvind Ltd

Date	Close Price	200 DMA	Change	% Variation
16-Sep-08	27.85	48.65	-20.80	-74.67
17-Sep-08	27.15	48.42	-21.27	-78.35
18-Sep-08	26.8	48.19	-21.39	-79.82
19-Sep-08	27.6	47.96	-20.36	-73.78
22-Sep-08	27.35	47.73	-20.38	-74.50

Chinki portfolio value=4663x27.60=128698.80 So now Chinki has a loss of 300000-128698.80= -171301.20 and Chandu hold his remaining cash 98560.46 plus he also get one-year saving market interest @4% for his cash holding, which was 3615.47 rupees for 19 Sept 2007 to 19 Sept 2008. On 19 Sept 2008:-

Chandu total cash was 98560.46 + 3615.47 = 102175.93 So what Chandu lost in 2008 biggest stock market fall?

Chandu invests 1 lac rupees and his loss recover through saving account interest on his cash holding; he enjoys a good sleep every night and not worried about his Arvind stock downtrend which makes new year low every month.

So what moral I want to say through this story?

Moral:- *It is far better to sit on cash instead of holding stocks in a downtrend, and This story teach you how to identify downtrend and uptrend in a stock with a simple technical ratio of 200 DMA.*

Now Chinki asked "Chandu, Can I book loss now?

"No No Chinki it is a foolish step if you book your loss after 2-3 year holding in loss because if stock revival again from here then you feel cheated?

" But I do not want to see my reducing net worth which reduces every day and now my net worth reduced from 4.22 Lac to 1.28 Lac only. How painful this? when you enjoy interest and peaceful sleep, I check my stock price per day and every time my heart is down when I see my stock making a new year low." Chinki takes out a deep breath.

"Oh, Chinki do not be disappointed you are a long term investor for 10+ year like Warren Buffet so why you feel worried for 3 years only?" Chandu asked.

"Chandu does not pinch salt on my burns, Now I forget about Warren buffet and think I sell my entire holding here and follow your sharegenius method in this stock,"Chinki said.

"OK, Chinki if you honestly want to follow this method then you may book your loss and start investment from your remaining cash as per Mahesh Kaushik method,"Chandu replied.

"But I have no enough courage to book this huge loss, so I wait two more months, and if stock, not revival again in coming 2 months then I book my loss." Chinki decided.

"But Chinki it is more danger if you wait 2 months and suppose what happen if your stock will fall more in coming 2 months? Chandu asked.

"In this situation, I discuss my situation in a TV program where famous technical analyst

Mr.XYZ replied investor questions and took my decision as this famous technical analyst Mr.XYZ suggest.

"Chinki, why not you discuss your situation with Mahesh Kaushik?"

"Chandu, he is very slow since last 8 months his software, not advice to buy again in Arvind stock, but my other friends make daily cash by playing intraday in stocks suggested by Mr.XYZ."

Chandu said "OK, good night Chinki" and start his bike.

10

Mr.XYZ Suggestion to Chinki

After 2 months, Arvind stock price down more and on 19 Nov 2008 Arvind stock closed on 13.98 only.

Chandu MS Excel Sheet of Sharegenius Software with Arvind Ltd

Date	Close Price	200 DMA	Change	% Variation
14-Nov-08	16.82	37.22	-20.40	-121.27
17-Nov-08	15.74	37.05	-21.31	-135.41
18-Nov-08	14.35	36.90	-22.55	-157.12
19-Nov-08	13.98	36.70	-22.72	-162.53
20-Nov-08	13.49	36.51	-23.02	-170.67
21-Nov-08	14.03	36.33	-22.30	-158.95

So Chinki do a phone call in a famous TV programme where Mr.XYZ resolve investor questions through his chart and Chinki asked him "Hello sir , I am Chinki I am a big fan of you sir, Sir I bought 4665 Arvind Mills stocks my average price was 64.33 rupee per share and stock now closed at 13.98 only so what to do now?

Mr.XYZ replied, " Stock seen weak on weekly charts and daily charts, RSI is negative and Yearly Chart show lower top and higher bottom situation so, I think further downside remains in this stock, and I suggest you exit at this level and book your loss."

The program host also put some salt on Chinki burn "Why not you put stop loss Chinki on your buying?"

Chinki cut the phone line because she has no answer that why she do not put a stop loss.

Next day Chinki sell all of his 4665 stocks @ 13.55 and get 63210.75 rupees. She lost her 236790 rupees in Arvind trade and said "good bye to stock market investing.

Now I want to say one thing.

Analyst on TV was not wrong because he says right that " Stock seen weak on weekly charts and daily charts, RSI is negative and Yearly Chart show lower top to the higher bottom situation so, I think further downside remains in this stock…"

He expresses his view for trading purpose and not given a fundamental advice for the 10-year view.

His chart reading is absolutely right because of this stock down from 13.98 to 11.20 in coming 4 months see this price of 12 March 2009:-

Chandu MS Excel Sheet of Sharegenius Software with Arvind Ltd

Date	Close Price	200 DMA	Change	% Variation
5-Mar-09	11.6	25.84	-14.24	-122.76
6-Mar-09	11.31	25.65	-14.34	-126.76
9-Mar-09	11.13	25.44	-14.31	-128.59
12-Mar-09	11.2	25.24	-14.04	-125.36
13-Mar-09	11.77	25.04	-13.27	-112.73

So analyst was not wrong Chinki understands his advice in the wrong manner.

11

When Chandu Reinvest In Arvind Ltd

Now 2nd half of this story start, Chinki booked her loss and decided that in future she never invest in the stock market because she thinks the stock market is dangerous for small investors.

Chandu continues to fill entries in my software every night Chandu fill close price in excel sheet and drag down the formula; it will hardly take 5 minutes per day.

If you are not able to spend your 5 minutes per day for fill up the formula in excel sheet, then this book is not for you. So stop reading here go to Amazon site and put a negative review that Mahesh Kaushik sells a third class idea to you. (I knew you do not do that because if you come on this page and read earlier story then it automatic clear that you have the capacity to digest this idea).

If you agree to spend 5 minutes per day for your excel software, then this 2nd half of this book lighting up your mind and no one stops you from becoming a millionaire in coming 10 years.

See your excel sheet which you download earlier you find that:-

Chandu MS Excel Sheet of Sharegenius Software with Arvind Ltd

Date	Close Price	200 DMA	Change	% Variation
15-May-09	18.4	20.48	-2.08	-11.29
18-May-09	20.95	20.42	0.53	2.54
19-May-09	19.65	20.36	-0.71	-3.61
20-May-09	23.25	20.32	2.93	12.61
21-May-09	24.45	20.28	4.17	17.04
22-May-09	26.3	20.26	6.04	22.98
25-May-09	27.95	20.24	7.71	27.59
26-May-09	26.55	20.21	6.34	23.88
27-May-09	31.8	20.20	11.60	36.48
28-May-09	32.15	20.19	11.96	37.20
29-May-09	34.2	20.19	14.01	40.97
1-Jun-09	33.2	20.18	13.02	39.23

On 18 May 2009 stock close 2.54% above from his 200 DMA, Stock traded below 200 DMA for a long period of 1 year 5 months.

But next day on 19 May 2009 stock again falls -3.61% below from 200 DMA.

20 May 2009 stock closed 12.61% above from his 200 DMA, so variation percentage from 200

DMA again come from (-)sign to (+) sign and as I tell in Chapter 6 of this book

" *Whenever your stock % variation from 200 DMA recover from (-) sign to (+) sign then every time you consider it as a starting point . it means if your stock recovers from(-)% variation below 200 DMA to (+)% variation above 200 DMA then you bought your one lot (start investing with one part of your money).* "

So Chandu invests INR 10,000 (Invest 2 part of his money one for 5% and second for 10% upside because of a stock close above 12.61% above from 200 DMA.

On 20 May 2009

Closed price 23.25

12.61 % above from 200 DMA

Time to order for 5%+ and 10%+ upside

Ordered 426 shares @23.48 (23.25+0.23)

So next day when the market opens on 21 May 2009 Chandu bought order executed by exchange and Chandu bought 426 shares on 21 May 2009.

Fresh investment=426x23.48=10002.48

Total share on 21 May 2009= 426

Remain Cash = 102175.93-10002.48=92173.45

For easy calculation, I ignore Brokerage on these examples.

When you see complete excel chart, then you see this stock continue up day by day from 20 MAY 2009 and within 8 days stock up 40% above from his 200 DMA.

I provide a picture for those readers who does not download complete Excel sheet yet:-

Chandu MS Excel Sheet of Sharegenius Software with Arvind Ltd

Date	Close Price	200 DMA	Change	% Variation
15-May-09	18.4	20.48	-2.08	-11.29
18-May-09	20.95	20.42	0.53	2.54
19-May-09	19.65	20.36	-0.71	-3.61
20-May-09	23.25	20.32	2.93	12.61
21-May-09	24.45	20.28	4.17	17.04
22-May-09	26.3	20.26	6.04	22.98
25-May-09	27.95	20.24	7.71	27.59
26-May-09	26.55	20.21	6.34	23.88
27-May-09	31.8	20.20	11.60	36.48
28-May-09	32.15	20.19	11.96	37.20
29-May-09	34.2	20.19	14.01	40.97
1-Jun-09	33.2	20.18	13.02	39.23

On 21 May 09

Closed price 24.45

17.04% above from 200 DMA

Time to order for 15% upside

Ordered 203 shares @24.69(24.45+0.24)

So next day when the market opens on 22 May 2009 Chandu bought order executed by exchange and Chandu bought 203 shares on 22 May 2009.

Fresh investment=203 x 24.69=5012.07

Total share on 22 May 09= 629

Remain Cash = 92173.45-5012.07=87161.38

For easy calculation, I ignore Brokerage on these examples.

On 22 May 09 Chandu hold total 629 Arvind shares and Market value of his holdings was 15530.01, So Chandu sit on a net profit of INR 515.46

On 22 May 09

Closed price 26.3

22.98% above from 200 DMA

Time to order for 20% upside

Ordered 189 shares @26.56(26.3+0.26)

23 May 09 and 24 May 09 were market holidays, so next trading day when the market opens on 25 May 2009 Chandu bought order executed by exchange and Chandu bought 189 shares on 25 May 2009.

Fresh investment=189 x 26.56=5019.84

Total share on 25 May 09= 818

Remain Cash = 87161.38-5019.84=82141.54

For easy calculation, I ignore Brokerage on these examples.

On 25 May 09 Chandu hold total 818 Arvind shares and Market value of his holdings was 21726.08, So Chandu sit on a net profit of INR 1691.69

On 25 May 09

Closed price 27.95

27.59% above from 200 DMA

Time to order for 25% upside

Ordered 177 shares @28.22(27.95+0.27)

On next trading day, Chandu order executed by the exchange.

Fresh investment=177 x 28.22=4994.94

Total share on 26 May 09= 995

Remain Cash = 82141.54-4994.94=77146.6

For easy calculation, I ignore Brokerage on these examples.

On 26 May 09 Chandu hold total 995 Arvind shares and Market value of his holdings was 28078.9, So Chandu sit on a net profit of INR 3049.57

__Increasing profit is the wonderful part of this method.__

__Every time you increase your holding with my method, your net profit also increase.__

On 27 May 09

Closed price 31.8

36.48% above from 200 DMA

Time to order for 30% and 35 % upside

Ordered 311 shares @32.11(31.8+0.31)

Order executed on 28 May 2009

Fresh investment=311 x 32.11=9986.21

Total share on 28 May 09= 1306

Remain Cash = 77146.6-9986.21=67160.39

For easy calculation, I ignore Brokerage on these examples.

On 28 May 09 Chandu hold total 1306 Arvind shares and Market value of his holdings was 41935.66, So Chandu sit on a net profit of INR 6920.12

On 29 May 09

Closed price 34.2

40.97% above from 200 DMA

Time to order for 40% upside

Ordered 145 shares @34.54(34.2+0.34)

30 and 31 May 2009 was market holidays, so order executed on 1 June 2009.

Fresh investment=145 x 34.54=5008.3

Total share on 01 June 09= 1451

Remain Cash = 67160.39-5008.3=62152.09

For easy calculation, I ignore Brokerage on these examples.

On 01 June 09 Chandu hold total 1451 Arvind shares and Market value of his holdings was 50117.54, So Chandu sit on a net profit of INR 10093.7

So whenever right time starts for fresh bought or sells your excel sheet, automatically tell you when to bought and when to sell.

And with method Chandu earn a safe profit of INR 10093.70 within 10 days.

Here I call this notional profit as "Safe Profit" because if the stock price falls again then excel sheet automatic trigger your selling points and you get exit with the minimum loss which not considers as a loss in my reverse trading system theory.

12

Reverse Trading System Theory

If you bought my earlier book and read Chapter 10 "Reverse Trading System" then you knew that as per this theory reverse trading might protect you from loss.

I write a summary of this system again for any new reader which not familiar with this theory.

When you are trapped in a loss-making the investment, then track his year high year low ratio when stock crash more than 50 % from his year high it means year high/ year low ratio is more than 2, so this is a sign of long-term bearish trend then sell it. And after some year when year high / year low ratio is less than 1.5, this time, you will buy your same quantity again.

Here in Chandu and Chinki book, we modified this reverse trading theory through 200 DMA which is more easy to track than year high/low.

Modified reverse trading system:- Sell one part of your stock every 5% fall from 200 DMA and bought again for every 5% rise from 200 DMA.

For example when Chandu holding of 557 Arvind shares fall from 200 DMA then he sells these stocks @ 46 and gets cash back of 25622 through this selling in loss:-

Chandu Balance Sheet from 19 Sept 2005				
Date	Buy	Price @	Total Inestment	Cash in hand
5-Sep-07	96	52.01	4992.96	99007.04
14-Sep-07	92	54.54	5017.68	93989.36
27-Sep-07	83	60.34	5008.22	93001.14
1-Oct-07	80	62.51	5000.8	88000.34
5-Oct-07	76	65.95	5012.2	82988.14
16-Oct-07	69	73.42	5065.98	77922.16
5-Dec-07	61	81.7	4983.7	72938.46
total	557		35081.54	
Date	sell	Price @	Total Amount get	
23-Jan-08	557	46	25622	98560.46
Net Loss			9459.54	

But when Arvind stock recover Chandu again bought these 557 stocks near 24 (read earlier chapter of this book again Chandu bought 476 stocks at 23.48 and 203 stocks at 24.69 so average price for 557 stocks near 24)

So Chandu gets cash back INR 25622 by selling of 557 stocks and bought this 557 share again with an investment of 557*24=13368.

So actually Chandu earn 25622-13368=12254 from this trade.

Initially, we feel Chandu book loss of INR 9459.54 when he sells his stock in the loss but actually, Chandu earn 12254 again from a reverse trade, so this loss is recovered from this trade.

If you trade with the help of my sharegenius trade system, then you invest only 5 minutes per day and enjoy a tension free safe investment in stocks but the story does not end here, we can continue our learning in next chapters.

13

Four Years Return of Chandu & Chinki

After 29 May 2009 Arvind Ltd stock price bound in range. Stock price fluctuates between a range of 21 to 37 till 16 September 2009.

So in these 3.5 months Chandu per day open his excel sheet, fill close price data, copy formula and, watch stock price % variation from 200 DMA, but chandu find that in these 3.5 months stock not rise more than 40% from 200 DMA and not fall below 200 DMA, so these 3.5 months is a silent zone for Chandu.

In these 3.5 months, he holds his 1451 Arvind shares and not bought and sell any share because his software does not indicate to bought or sell.

Kindly refer your excel sheet which you download earlier.

On 17 September 2009 Arvind stock closed 45.54% above from 200 DMA, so this is the time to fill up an order for 45%+ upside.

See this picture for understanding 17 September 2009 situation:-

Chandu MS Excel Sheet of Sharegenius Software with Arvind Ltd

Date	Close Price	200 DMA	Change	% Variation
14-Sep-09	34.85	20.97	13.88	39.83
15-Sep-09	35.25	21.08	14.17	40.21
16-Sep-09	37.2	21.19	16.01	43.03
17-Sep-09	39.15	21.32	17.83	45.54
18-Sep-09	38.75	21.44	17.31	44.66
22-Sep-09	38.7	21.57	17.13	44.27
23-Sep-09	37.1	21.68	15.42	41.55

On 17 Sept 09

Closed price 39.15

45.54% above from 200 DMA

Time to order for 45% upside

Ordered 127 shares @39.54(39.15+0.39)

On next trading day (18 Sept 09) Chandu order executed and Chandu bought 127 Shares.

Fresh investment=127 x 39.54=5021.58

Total share on 18 Sept 09= 1578

Remain Cash = 62152.09-5021.58=57130.51

For easy calculation, I ignore Brokerage on these examples.

On 18 Sept 09, Chandu hold total 1578 Arvind shares and Market value of his holdings was 62394.12, So Chandu sit on a net profit of INR 17348.70

On 19 Sept 2009 total 4 years of Chandu and Chinki investments are complete, and Chandu also gets INR 3520.01 as 4% saving account interest for last year.

Chandu invited Chinki for review their last 4 year investments.

Chandu said " Chinki; Now I am holding 1578 Stocks of Arvind Ltd which market value is 62394.12 and my total cash is 60650.52 (57130.51+3520.01 saving as interest) So my net worth is 123044.64.

Chinki replied, "That's good Chandu, but I think you may book your profit here because if the market falls again then all of your profit gone like Jan 2008."

"No Chinki, I think you may start investing again because if your dream really becomes true, then you easily recover your loss of 236790 rupees."

" No Chandu now I say goodbye to the stock market, and I think CMP 39 is so high for this stock because of just few month ago this stock traded @12, and I think the stock may fall below 12 again then I review my decision, and maybe start investing again if this stock available below 12.

Overall Chinki does not agree to start investing again, and Chandu does not agree to book profit and break discipline of my software.

Let's see what happen in coming years.

14

Recovery from Minus Sign to Plus Sign is a Fresh Starting Point

From 19 Sept 2009 to 12 March, 2010 Arvind Ltd again trade in a range bound movement.

So in these 6 months stock not break 50%+above from 200 DMA which was Chandu next level to bought or not break his 200 DMA to the downside.

Unfortunately, on 15 March 2010 Stock closed at 33.25 which is 1.5% below from 200 DMA, Refer your excel sheet of look this picture:-

Chandu MS Excel Sheet of Sharegenius Software with Arvind Ltd

Date	Close Price	200 DMA	Change	% Variation
12-Mar-10	33.8	33.72	0.08	0.23
15-Mar-10	33.25	33.75	-0.50	-1.50
16-Mar-10	33.85	33.78	0.07	0.19
17-Mar-10	33.65	33.79	-0.14	-0.43
18-Mar-10	34.65	33.81	0.84	2.44
19-Mar-10	35.7	33.81	1.89	5.28
22-Mar-10	34.5	33.82	0.68	1.97

So Chandu waits -5% closing point for start selling but before this point will come stock price was rise again, and the stock closed 5.28% above on 19 March 2010.

If you seriously read this book, then you remember that in Chapter 6 fo this book I told that:-

" _**Whenever your stock % variation from 200 DMA recover from (-) sign to (+) sign then every time you consider it as a starting point . it means if your stock recovers from -% variation below 200 DMA to +% variation above 200 DMA then you bought your one lot (start investing with one part of your money).**_ "

So as per this rule, Chandu ordered a fresh lot for 5%+ upside:-

On 19 March 10

Closed price 35.7

5.28% above from 200 DMA

Time to order for 5% fresh upside

Ordered 139 shares @36.05(35.7+0.35)

On next trading day, (22 March 10) Chandu order executed and Chandu bought 139 Shares.

Fresh investment=139 x 36.05=5010.95

Total share on 22 March 10= 1717

Remain Cash = 60650.52-5010.95=55639.57

For easy calculation, I ignore Brokerage on these examples.

On 22 March 10, Chandu hold total 1717 Arvind shares and Market value of his holdings was 61897.85, So Chandu sits on a net profit of INR 11841.48.

Same happen on 21 Apr 2010 when stock recovers from minus sign to plus sign and closed 5.07 % above from 200 DMA.

We consider it as a fresh entry point because whenever this situation happens, it indicates technicals of stock will strong, and we need to invest more amount.

See a picture of 21 Apr 2010 situation:-

Chandu MS Excel Sheet of Sharegenius Software with Arvind Ltd

Date	Close Price	200 DMA	Change	% Variation
15-Apr-10	34.1	34.04	0.06	0.17
16-Apr-10	33.65	34.07	-0.42	-1.24
19-Apr-10	33.1	34.10	-1.00	-3.01
20-Apr-10	33.75	34.13	-0.38	-1.13
21-Apr-10	36	34.18	1.82	5.07
22-Apr-10	35.85	34.22	1.63	4.56

So as per rule on 21 Apr Chandu ordered 138 more shares.

On 21 Apr 10

Closed price 36

5.07% above from 200 DMA

Time to order for 5% fresh upside

Ordered 138 shares @36.36(36+0.36)

On next trading day (22 Apr 10) Chandu order executed and Chandu bought 138 Shares.

Fresh investment=138 x 36.36=5017.68

Total share on 22 Apr 10= 1855

Remain Cash = 55639.57-5017.68=50621.89

For easy calculation, I ignore Brokerage on these examples.

On 22 Apr 10, Chandu hold total 1855 Arvind shares and Market value of his holdings was 67447.8, So Chandu sit on a net profit of INR 12373.75

I hope that you will catch the point that every time when stock variation from 200 DMA recover from (-) sign to (+) sign, we consider it as fresh entry level.

15

Situation in May 2010 Stock Market Fall

In May 2010 Indian stock market fall again and as per market movement Arvind, the stock also falls -5% or more below from his 200 DMA.

So in this chapter, we learn that how Chandu booked his profits during that stock market fall of May 2010 where normal investor crying to see their losses and Chandu smile to see his profits.

Look at this situation of Arvind Ltd Share from 5 May 2010 to 29 May 2010:-

Chandu MS Excel Sheet of Sharegenius Software with Arvind Ltd

Date	Close Price	200 DMA	Change	% Variation
5-May-10	34.7	34.67	0.03	0.10
6-May-10	34	34.73	-0.73	-2.14
7-May-10	32.9	34.78	-1.88	-5.72
10-May-10	33.9	34.83	-0.93	-2.74
11-May-10	33.6	34.88	-1.28	-3.80
12-May-10	33.2	34.92	-1.72	-5.18
13-May-10	33.2	34.96	-1.76	-5.30
14-May-10	33	35.00	-2.00	-6.06
17-May-10	32.85	35.04	-2.19	-6.67
18-May-10	32.6	35.07	-2.47	-7.59
19-May-10	32.65	35.10	-2.45	-7.51
20-May-10	32.1	35.12	-3.02	-9.42
21-May-10	31.55	35.14	-3.59	-11.39
24-May-10	31.9	35.17	-3.27	-10.25
25-May-10	30.55	35.19	-4.63	-15.17
26-May-10	30.6	35.20	-4.60	-15.03

On 7 May 2010 Arvind stock closed @32.90 which was 5.72% below from 200 DMA so as per our rule For every 5% downfall from 200 DMA, we sell our one lot (one part).

If the stock falls 10% from 200 DMA, then we sell another part.

If the stock falls 15% from 200 DMA, then we sell our 3rd part as first come first serve policy we sell our oldest buying first.

So Chandu put an off-market sell order for his first lot.

Whenever you put an off-market sell order then always put 1 % lower price in limit price because if any stock is technically weak then it may be possible a gap up opening in next trading session and if next day stock opens below earlier close price and price do not rise again during market time then you lost your selling opportunity.

Ok, I think you may forget about Chandu first lot, See Sheet 2 in your downloaded sheet where I provide Chandu Complete balance Sheet.

If you do not download Excel sheet, then refer this picture to remember Chandu buyings and identify which lot Chandu sell on next trading session.

Date	Buy	Price @	Total Inestment	Saving Ac Interest	Dividend gain	Cash in hand
19-Sep-08	-	-	-	3615.47	-	102175.93
21-May-09	426	23.48	10002.48	-	-	92173.45
22-May-09	203	24.69	5012.07	-	-	87161.38
25-May-09	189	26.56	5019.84	-	-	82141.54
26-May-09	177	28.22	4994.94	-	-	77146.6
28-May-09	311	32.11	9986.21	-	-	67160.39
1-Jun-09	145	34.54	5008.3	-	-	62152.09
18-Sep-09	127	39.54	5021.58	-	-	57130.51
19-Sep-09	-	-	-	3520.01	-	60650.52
22-Mar-10	139	36.05	5010.95	-	-	55639.57
22-Apr-10	138	36.36	5017.68	-	-	50621.89

According to above balance sheet on 21, May 2016 Chandu bought 426 shares as two lot, one for 5% upside and second for 10% upside, so 426/2=213 shares considered as the first lot.

On 07 May 10

Closed price 32.90

-5.72 % below from 200 DMA

Sell 213 Shares

Ordered Price= Ordered Price=32.58 (last close 32.90-0.32) I think you remember when we put off-market sell order then always put price 1% below from closing price.

On next trading day, 10 May 10 Chandu order executed and Chandu sells his 213 Shares.

Total amount get=213 x32.58 =6939.54 Rupees

Principal Amount of these 213 Shares=213x23.48=5001.24 Rupees

Net Profit=6939.54-5001.24=1938.30 Rupees

Remain Share = 1642

Remain Cash = 50621.89+6939.54 =57561.43 Rupees

Total Booked Profit=1938.3 Rupees

For easy calculation, I ignore Brokerage on these examples.

On 21 May 10

Closed price 31.55

-11.39 % below from 200 DMA

Time to sell order for oldest buying So here the oldest lot was 213 Shares Which he bought on 21 May 09.(Refer Balance sheet in excel sheet on 21 May 09 Chandu bought 2 lot and bought total 426 shares @23.48 , So here we consider 426/2=213 shares.)

Sell 213 Shares

Ordered Price=31.24 (last close 31.55-0.31) I think you remember when we put off-market sell order then always put price 1% below from closing price.

On next trading day, 24 May 10 Chandu order executed and Chandu sells his 213 Shares.

Total amount get=213 x31.24 =6654.12 Rupees

Principal Amount of these 213 Shares=213x23.48=5001.24 Rupees

Net Profit=6654.12-5001.24=1652.88 Rupees

Remain Share = 1429

Remain Cash = 57561.43+6654.12 =64215.55 Rupees

Total Booked Profit=3591.18 Rupees

For easy calculation, I ignore Brokerage on these examples.

Date	sell	Price @	Total Amount get		Remain Cash
10-May-10	213	32.58	6939.54		57561.43
24-May-10	213	31.24	6654.12		64215.55
26-May-10	203	30.25	6140.75		70356.3

On 25 May 10

Closed price 30.55

-15.17 % below from 200 DMA

Time to sell order for oldest buying So here the oldest lot was 203 Shares Which he bought on 22 May 09.(Refer Balance sheet in excel sheet on 22 May 09 Chandu bought 203 shares @24.69 ,

So here we consider these 203 shares as the oldest lot.)

Sell 203 Shares

Ordered Price=30.25 (last close 30.55-0.30) I think you remember when we put off-market sell order then always put price 1% below from closing price.

On next trading day, 26 May 10 Chandu order executed and Chandu sells his 203 Shares.

Total amount get=203 x30.25 =6140.75 Rupees

Principal Amount for these 203 Shares=203x24.69=5012.07 Rupees

Net Profit=6140.75-5012.07=1128.68 Rupees

Remain Share = 1226

Remain Cash = 64215.55+6140.75 =70356.3 Rupees

Total Booked Profit=4719.86 Rupees

For easy calculation, I ignore Brokerage on these examples.

What we learn from above examples:- In above examples, you see that whenever stock price fall below his 200 DMA.

Then every -5% fall from 200 DMA, -10% fall from 200 DMA, -15% fall from 200 DMA or more level of five multiples my software automatic trigger oldest lot for a sell order.

Most of the time your oldest lot was 1 year or more old, so you no need to pay short term capital gain tax on this profit booking.

This profit booking also increases our cash which we utilized again when the price of a stock rise again.

So in this method, you automatic knew when to buy or when to sell a stock.

So instead of one-time investment for 5-10 year use this sharegenius software for a safe investment with maximized return.

In next chapter, we compare 5 years gain of Chandu and Chinki.

16

Compersion of 5 Years Gain

After May 2010 Stock market fall, Stock of Arvind Ltd rose again and closed 5% above from 200 DMA on 5 Aug 2010, So before we compare 19 Sept 2010 situation when 5 Year of Chandu and Chinki investment completed, I give you a quick look about Chandu fresh bought.

On 05 Aug 10

Closed price 37.15

5.10% above from 200 DMA

Time to order for 5% fresh upside

Ordered 134 shares @37.52(37.15+0.37)

On next trading day (6 Aug 10) Chandu order executed and Chandu bought 134 Shares.

Fresh investment=134 x 37.52=5027.68

Total share on 6 Aug 10= 1360

Remain Cash = 70356.30-5027.68=65328.62

For easy calculation, I ignore Brokerage on these examples.

On 6 Aug 10, Chandu holds total 1360 Arvind shares and Market value of his holdings was 51027.2, So Chandu sits on an unrealized profit of INR 5939.47.

Chandu unrealized profit=INR 5939.47

Realized profit=INR 4719.86

Total Profit on 6 Aug 10=INR 10659.33

On 10 Aug 10

Closed price 39.4

10.59% above from 200 DMA

Time to order for 10% fresh upside

Ordered 126 shares @39.79(39.4+0.39)

On next trading day (11 Aug 10) Chandu order executed and Chandu bought 126 Shares.

Fresh investment=126 x 39.79=5013.54

Total share on 11 Aug 10= 1486

Remain Cash = 65328.62-5013.54=60315.08

For easy calculation, I ignore Brokerage on these examples.

On 11 Aug 10, Chandu hold total 1486 Arvind shares and Market value of his holdings was 59127.94, So Chandu sits on an unrealized profit of INR 9026.67.

Chandu unrealized profit=INR 9026.67

Realized profit=INR 4719.86

Total Profit on 11 Aug 10=INR 13746.53

On 17 Aug 10

Closed price 43.1

17.99% above from 200 DMA

Time to order for 15% fresh upside

Ordered 115 shares @43.53(43.1+0.43)

On next trading day (18 Aug 10) Chandu order executed and Chandu bought 115 Shares.

Fresh investment=115 x 43.53=5005.95

Total share on 18 Aug 10= 1601

Remain Cash = 60315.08-5005.95=55309.13

For easy calculation, I ignore Brokerage on these examples.

On 18 Aug 10, Chandu hold total 1601 Arvind shares and Market value of his holdings was 69691.53, So Chandu sits on an unrealized profit of INR 14584.31.

Chandu unrealized profit=INR 14584.31

Realized profit=INR 4719.86

Total Profit on 18 Aug 10=INR 19304.17

On 07 Sep 10

Closed price 45

20.19% above from 200 DMA

Time to order for 20% fresh upside

Ordered 110 shares @45.45(45+0.45)

On next trading day (08 Sep 10) Chandu order executed and Chandu bought 110 Shares.

Fresh investment=110 x 45.45=4999.5

Total share on 08 Sep 10= 1711

Remain Cash = 55309.13-4999.5=50309.63

For easy calculation I ignore Brokerage on these examples.

On 08 Sep 10, Chandu hold total 1711 Arvind shares and Market value of his holdings was 77764.95, So Chandu sits on an unrealized profit of INR 17658.23.

Chandu unrealized profit=INR 17658.23

Realized profit=INR 4719.86

Total Profit on 08 Sep 10=INR 22378.09

Interest Income:- On 19 Sept 2010 next one year (total 5 years) completed so this is the time to add 4% saving account interest on Chandu cash holding.

I calculated saving account interest on minimum monthly amount of saving account so for 20 Sept 2009 to 19 Sept 2010 this 4% interest was=2412.47

So after this interest income, on 19 Sept 2010 Chandu cash holding was 50309.63+2412.47=52722.10

So Since last 5 years, Chandu earn INR 22378.09 from Arvind Stock and 17567.95 as saving account interest, so total gain since last 5 year was 22378.09+17568.95=39947.04

If Chandu invested a lump sum amount 1 lac in Arvind Stock on 19 Sept 2005 and bought 710 shares like Chinki then what happen?.

If he not uses my software and still holds 710 Share then what he get ?

In this situation after 5-year holding a market value of Chandu, 710 shares were 710*45.20=32092 only, and he holds only 710 shares since last 5 years.

But after using my technique, he earns 39947.04 and holds 1711 shares instead of 710 shares.

So these 5 years 2005 to 2010 was a bear cycle for Arvind Ltd where stock price down from 160 to 12 and recover till 45 only.

So from this story, you learn that what happened if you use my technic in a bear cycle of stock.

But main part of this story is still remain where you see how effective this technic in bull cycle of Arvind Stock where Chinki dream change into reality and Arvind Mills stocks touch the price of INR 415 and not only touch this high price stock of Arvind Mills demerger in two separate companies one name is Arvind Ltd the second name is Arvind infrastructure Ltd.

Some of the readers think that Chandu has only 52722.10 in cash so If he bought more and more shares till 415 rises then Chandu cash was finished, and after 10 lots he has no cash for fresh bought.

But this formula is so automatic that in every short downtrend of stock price formula suggest profit booking and this profit booking increase our cash which we utilized again when the price of stock rise again.

I think now you feel boring, So I will tell you an interesting story of a waiter who serves Icecream to Chandu and Chinki.

17

Investment of A Waiter Who Serves Icecream to Chandu and Chinki

This is a side story of this book. You knew Chandu and Chinki like ice cream cones, and they often enjoy ice cream cones in "Chamunda Café and Ice Cream Corner."

There was a waiter "Ghisu Bhai" who was also interested in the stock market, and Ghisu Bhai only checks his luck in intraday and cash market.

Ghisu Bhai knew that Chandu and Chinki also trade in stock market. So when he serve ice cream cone to Chandu and Chinki , he stopped a movement and tried to hear Chandu and Chinki debate.

He hears about Chinki dream, and he also wanted to buy some stocks of Arvind Mills, but in 2005 when he saw a high price of 140, he not collect sufficient brave to invest at this level.

When stock market fall in 2008 he noted that Arvind stock now comes down from 140 to 46 he thinks stock already down 67%, and he does not want to lose this Chance.

Because Ghisu Bhai also believe in dreams and he thinks Mata Ji (Goddess Durga) give him a chance to become a millionaire through the stock market.

So on 23 Jan 2008 trading session when Chandu sell his 557 stocks @46 , Same day Ghisu Bhai also put a bought order for 600 Stocks of Arvind Mills @46.

Oh No, As a coincident Exchange sell Chandu 557 stocks to Ghisu Bhai.

On 23 Jan 2008, Ghisu Bhai invest 600x46=INR 27600 in Arvind Share and on 12 March 2009 Stock fall till level of 11.20

So market value of Ghisu Bhai 600 stocks was 6720 only, and he is to a notional loss of INR 20880, but Ghisu Bhai thinks I am not a foolish like Chinki who sell her stocks in the loss, I believe in buy right sit tight theory.

Ghisu Bhai not realized his loss on 12 March 2009 and continued to hold them.

After a long wait of 2 years and 8 months on 15 Sept 2010, Arvind closed on 46.35, and he does not sell his stock he thinks I hold this stock near 3 years If I sell on no profit no loss then what it earn in these 3 years?

So Ghisu Bhai cleverly decided to hold this stock with trailing stop loss.

Unfortunately stock enter in downtrend again, and on 22 Sept 2015 Arvind closed @42.65, Now Ghisu Bhai again in the loss.

Ghisu Bhai change his strategy and think "If 46 come again then this time I sell it and shift to "Suzlon Energy" stock which is looking more promising and reasonably priced?

Luck always support Ghisu Bhai and Price of Arvind Ltd (Arvind mills name is changed to Arvind Ltd on 27 June 2008) rise again on 01 Oct 2010 and Ghisu Bhai sell his 600 stocks at no profit no loss.

Now Ghisu Bhai cleverly shifts his money in Suzlon Energy and on 01 Oct 2010 he bought 500 Shares of Suzlon Energy @55 per share.

I write this story on 1 Jan 2017, and since last 6 years Suzlon share not rise to price 55 and today price of Suzlon Energy is 13.94 Ghisu Bhai is very clever, and he still waits for his price 55 again for an exit in no profit no loss.

I think you catch the point behind this story and match your investment style with Chandu, Chinki, and Ghisu Bhai.

If your investment style is matched with Chinki or Ghisu Bhai, then please change your style of investment to Chandu style.

This is the main motto of this book.

18

Short Brief Of Chandu Buying Till 15 Dec 2011

If you read last 17 chapters of this book, you understand about my idea.Here I give a short brief of Chandu buying in Arvind Ltd shares till 15 Dec 2011.

Chandu MS Excel Sheet of Sharegenius Software with Arvind Ltd

Date	Close Price	200 DMA	Change	% Variation
13-Oct-10	51.45	36.98	14.47	28.13
14-Oct-10	49.8	37.03	12.77	25.64
15-Oct-10	51.1	37.09	14.01	27.42
18-Oct-10	52	37.16	14.85	28.55
19-Oct-10	56	37.24	18.76	33.51
20-Oct-10	54.5	37.31	17.19	31.54
21-Oct-10	53.85	37.39	16.46	30.57
22-Oct-10	54.35	37.45	16.90	31.10
25-Oct-10	56.95	37.52	19.43	34.12
26-Oct-10	55.6	37.59	18.01	32.40
27-Oct-10	58.95	37.68	21.27	36.08
28-Oct-10	59	37.77	21.23	35.98
29-Oct-10	57.7	37.86	19.84	34.39
1-Nov-10	58.6	37.95	20.65	35.25
2-Nov-10	58.85	38.04	20.81	35.36
3-Nov-10	59.85	38.14	21.71	36.28
4-Nov-10	60.3	38.24	22.06	36.59
5-Nov-10	60.9	38.34	22.56	37.04
8-Nov-10	62.85	38.45	24.40	38.82
9-Nov-10	64.3	38.57	25.73	40.01
10-Nov-10	66.2	38.72	27.48	41.51

It is recommended that you refer Excel sheet which you download earlier and match the data given here.

On 13 Oct 10

Closed price 51.45

28.13% above from 200 DMA

Time to order for 25% fresh upside

Ordered 97 shares @51.96(51.45+0.51)

On next trading day, (14 Oct 10) Chandu order executed and Chandu bought 97 Shares.

Fresh investment=97 x 51.96=5040.12

Total shares on 14 Oct 10= 1808

Remain Cash = 52722.1-5040.12=47681.98

For easy calculation, I ignore Brokerage on these examples.

On 14 Oct 10

Chandu total Arvind shares= 1808

Market price per shares=51.96

Market value =1808x51.96= 93943.68

Net worth=Cash 47681.98+ Market value of Shares 93943.68=141625.66

On 19 Oct 10

Closed price 56

33.51% above from 200 DMA

Time to order for30% fresh upside

Ordered 89 shares @56.56(56+0.56)

On next trading day, (20 Oct 2010) Chandu order executed and Chandu bought 89 shares.

Fresh investment=89 x 56.56=5033.84

Total shares on 40471= 1897

Remain Cash = 47681.98-5033.84=42648.14

For easy calculation, I ignore Brokerage on these examples.

On 20 Oct 10

Chandu total Arvind shares= 1897

Market price per shares=56.56

Market value =1897x56.56= 107294.32

Net worth=Cash 42648.14+ Market value of Shares107294.32=149942.46

On 27 Oct 10

Closed price 58.95

36.08% above from 200 DMA

Time to order for 35% fresh upside

Ordered 84 shares @59.53(58.95+0.58)

On next trading day, (28 Oct 10) Chandu order executed and Chandu bought 84 shares.

Fresh investment=84 x 59.53=5000.52

Total shares on 28 Oct 10= 1981

Remain Cash = 42648.14-5000.52=37647.62

For easy calculation, I ignore Brokerage on these examples.

On 28 Oct 10

Chandu total Arvind shares= 1981

Market price per shares=59.53

Market value =1981x59.53= 117928.93

Net worth=Cash 37647.62+ Market value of Shares117928.93=155576.55

On 09 Nov 10

Closed price 64.3

40.01% above from 200 DMA

Time to order for 40% fresh upside

Ordered 77 shares @64.94(64.3+0.64)

On next trading day (10 Nov 10) Chandu order executed and Chandu bought 77 Shares.

Fresh investment=77 x 64.94=5000.38

Total shares on 10 Nov 10= 2058

Remain Cash = 37647.62-5000.38=32647.24

For easy calculation, I ignore Brokerage on these examples.

On 10 Nov 10

Chandu total Arvind shares= 2058

Market price per shares=64.94

Market value =2058x64.94= 133646.52

Net worth=Cash 32647.24+ Market value of Shares133646.52=166293.76

On Aug 2011 Stock again fell below his 200 DMA So when the stock price rises again, Chandu again start fresh buying from 5%+ upside.

Chandu MS Excel Sheet of Sharegenius Software with Arvind Ltd

Date	Close Price	200 DMA	Change	% Variation
18-Aug-11	65.5	68.37	-2.87	-4.38
19-Aug-11	67.6	68.41	-0.81	-1.20
22-Aug-11	70.55	68.47	2.08	2.95
23-Aug-11	73.45	68.53	4.92	6.70
24-Aug-11	74.45	68.60	5.85	7.86

On 23 Aug 11

Closed price 73.45

6.70% above from 200 DMA

Time to order for 05% fresh upside

Ordered 68 shares @74.18(73.45+0.73)

On next trading day, (24 Aug 11) Chandu order executed and Chandu bought 68 shares.

Fresh investment=68 x 74.18=5044.24

Total shares on 24 Aug 11= 2126

Remain Cash = 32647.24-5044.24=27603

For easy calculation, I ignore Brokerage on these examples.

On 24 Aug 11

Chandu total Arvind shares= 2126

Market price per shares=74.18

Market value =2126x74.18= 157706.68

Net worth=Cash 27603+ Market value of Shares157706.68=185309.68

Chandu MS Excel Sheet of Sharegenius Software with Arvind Ltd				
Date	Close Price	200 DMA	Change	% Variation
30-Aug-11	78.35	68.82	9.53	12.17
2-Sep-11	80.85	68.91	11.94	14.77
5-Sep-11	83.65	69.03	14.62	17.48
6-Sep-11	82.75	69.16	13.59	16.42
7-Sep-11	82.75	69.29	13.46	16.27
8-Sep-11	85.2	69.44	15.76	18.50
9-Sep-11	91.9	69.61	22.29	24.25
12-Sep-11	93.5	69.80	23.70	25.35
13-Sep-11	90.55	69.98	20.57	22.71

On 30 Aug 11

Closed price 78.35

12.17% above from 200 DMA

Time to order for 10% fresh upside

Ordered 64 shares @79.13(78.35+0.78)

On next trading day, (02 Sept 11) Chandu order executed and Chandu bought 64 Shares.

Fresh investment=64 x 79.13=5064.32

Total shares on 02 Sept 11= 2190

Remain Cash = 27603-5064.32=22538.68

For easy calculation, I ignore Brokerage on these examples.

On 02 Sept 11

Chandu total Arvind shares= 2190

Market price per shares=79.13

Market value =2190x79.13= 173294.7

Net worth=Cash 22538.68+ Market value of Shares173294.7=195833.38

On 5 Sept 11

Closed price 83.65

17.48% above from 200 DMA

Time to order for 15% fresh upside

Ordered 60 shares @84.48(83.65+0.83)

On next trading day, (06 Sept 11) Chandu order executed and Chandu bought 60 Shares.

Fresh investment=60 x 84.48=5068.8

Total shares on 06 Sept 11= 2250

Remain Cash = 22538.68-5068.8=17469.88

For easy calculation, I ignore Brokerage on these examples.

On 06 Sept 11

Chandu total Arvind shares= 2250

Market price per shares=84.48

Market value =2250x84.48= 190080

Net worth=Cash 17469.88+ Market value of Shares190080=207549.88

On 9 Sept 11

Closed price 91.9

24.25% above from 200 DMA

Time to order for 20% fresh upside

Ordered 54 shares @92.81(91.9+0.91)

On next trading day, (12 Sept 11) Chandu order executed and Chandu bought 54 Shares.

Fresh investment=54 x 92.81=5011.74

Total shares on 12 Sept 11= 2304

Remain Cash = 17469.88-5011.74=12458.14

For easy calculation, I ignore Brokerage on these examples.

On 12 Sept 11

Chandu total Arvind shares= 2304

Market price per shares=92.81

Market value =2304x92.81= 213834.24

Net worth=Cash 12458.14+ Market value of Shares213834.24=226292.38

On 12 Sept 11

Closed price 93.5

25.35% above from 200 DMA

Time to order for 25% fresh upside

Ordered 53 shares @94.43(93.5+0.93)

On next trading day, (13 Sept 11) Chandu order executed and Chandu bought 53 Shares.

Fresh investment=53 x 94.43=5004.79

Total shares on 13 Sept 11= 2357

Remain Cash = 12458.14-5004.79=7453.35

For easy calculation, I ignore Brokerage on these examples.

On 13 Sept 11

Chandu total Arvind shares= 2357

Market price per shares=94.43

Market value =2357x94.43= 222571.51

Net worth=Cash 7453.35+ Market value of shares222571.51=230024.86

Saving Account Interest on 19 Sept 2011:- On 19 Sept 2011 six years of Chandu and Chinki investment story is completed. Chandu gets INR 1364.60 as last year saving account interest.

As the price of Arvind rise, Chandu increases his holding as per my recommended method.

As Chandu increase equity portion his cash holding is decreased so this year, Chandu gets only 1364.60 as 4% saving account interest on his cash holding for last year.

Now Remain Cash=7453.35+1364.60=8817.95

On 14 Oct 11

Closed price 106.4

30.06% above from 200 DMA

Time to order for30% fresh upside

Ordered 47 shares @107.46(106.4+1.06)

On next trading day, (17 Oct 11) Chandu order executed and Chandu bought 47 shares.

Fresh investment=47 x 107.46=5050.62

Total shares on 17 Oct 11= 2404

Remain Cash = 8817.95-5050.62=3767.33

For easy calculation, I ignore Brokerage on these examples.

On 17 Oct 11

Chandu total Arvind shares= 2404

Market price per shares=107.46

Market value =2404x107.46= 258333.84

Net worth=Cash 3767.33+ Market value of Shares258333.84=262101.17

I think you remember that Chinki initially bought 710 shares @ 140.85 and invest near 1 lac.

Price of Arvind Ltd is still below from Chinki buying price 140.85

If Chinki still holds her 710 shares, then market value of her shares is 710x107.46= INR 76296.60, but Chandu net worth is rising INR 262101.17 with my method and story is still remain.

19

How Downfall Refill Chandu Cash With Tax-Free Profits

At the end of the earlier chapter, you see Chandu almost utilized his cash to buy Arvind shares. Now Chandu has only INR 3767.33 remains in cash, and if stock further rises from here for 35%+upside from 200 DMA, then Chandu has no cash for bought.

But stocks do not move one-sided after a long rise correction happens, and Chandu is lucky that Arvind Ltd Stock correct from 12 Dec 2011 and you wonder that Stock correct from the price of 108.65 (Price at 19 Oct 11) to 65 (Price at 2 Jan 12).

So my sharegenius software automatic suggests profit booking in this downfall.

In this chapter, you see how this profit-booking secure Chandu profit and refill Chandu cash for further buying.

I knew you have one question that If Arvind stock not falls at this point and rise more from here, then how Chandu bought his next lot because now his remain cash is 3767.33 only which is insufficient for next lot.

However, profit booking starts on just this break event point where Chandu all cash is utilized, but if the stock price rises more from here, then Chandu need only 5000-3767=1233 rupees for fresh buying.

When you buy on the rise, then your profit always increase with every fresh buying, On 17 Oct 2011 Chandu sit on a net profit of INR 162000.

So when you sit on a profit of 162000, then it is not hard to invest 1233 fresh money in continuing your profit increasing system.

But fortunately Chandu no need to inject fresh money into his system because profit booking is start and this profit booking refill Chandu cash.

Refer you excel sheet or this picture for the situation on Dec 2011:-

Chandu MS Excel Sheet of Sharegenius Software with Arvind Ltd

Date	Close Price	200 DMA	Change	% Variation
12-Dec-11	80.55	80.48	0.07	0.09
13-Dec-11	79.9	80.59	-0.69	-0.86
14-Dec-11	78.85	80.70	-1.85	-2.34
15-Dec-11	76.65	80.79	-4.14	-5.40
16-Dec-11	69.1	80.85	-11.75	-17.01
19-Dec-11	70.25	80.93	-10.68	-15.20
20-Dec-11	70.2	81.01	-10.81	-15.40
21-Dec-11	72.9	81.10	-8.20	-11.25
22-Dec-11	73.4	81.18	-7.78	-10.60
23-Dec-11	71.4	81.25	-9.85	-13.80
26-Dec-11	72.9	81.34	-8.44	-11.57
27-Dec-11	69.8	81.41	-11.61	-16.64
28-Dec-11	67.05	81.48	-14.43	-21.52
29-Dec-11	66.9	81.53	-14.63	-21.86
30-Dec-11	66.7	81.58	-14.88	-22.30
2-Jan-12	64.95	81.63	-16.68	-25.68
3-Jan-12	69.25	81.69	-12.44	-17.96

I think you remember that for every 5% downfall from 200 DMA, we sell our one lot (one part).
If the stock falls 10% from 200 DMA, then we sell another part.

If the stock falls 15% from 200 DMA, then we sell our 3rd part as first come first serve policy we sell our oldest buying first.

See Sheet 2 of your Excel sheet where I give balance sheet of Chandu bought and sold so as per this sheet you knew that these oldest buyings are available for selling;-

Date	Buy	Price @	Total Inestment	Saving Ac Interest	Dividend gain.	Cash in hand
25-May-09	189	26.56	5019.84	-	-	82141.54
26-May-09	177	28.22	4994.94	-	-	77146.6
28-May-09	311	32.11	9986.21	-	-	67160.39
1-Jun-09	145	34.54	5008.3	-	-	62152.09
18-Sep-09	127	39.54	5021.58	-	-	57130.51

On 15 Dec 11

Closed price 78.85

-5.4 % below from 200 DMA

Time to book profit in oldest buying.

 So here oldest buying lot was 189 Shares Which he bought on 25 May 09.(Refer Balance sheet in excel sheet on 25 May 09 Chandu bought 189 shares @26.56 , Which we consider as the oldest lot.)

Chandu fill sell order for 189 Shares

Ordered Price=78.07 (last close 78.85-0.78) I think you remember when we put off-market sell order then always put price 1% below from closing price.

On next trading day, 16 Dec 11 Chandu order executed and Chandu sells his 189 Shares.

Total amount get=189 x78.07 =14755.23 Rupees

Principal Amount for these 189 Shares=189x26.56=5019.84 Rupees

Net Profit=14755.23-5019.84=9735.39 Rupees

Remain Shares = 2215

Market Value of Remain Shares=2215x78.07=172925.05

Remain Cash =3767.33+14755.23 =18522.56 Rupees

Net worth on 16 Dec 11 = Cash 18522.56+ Market value of remain 2215 shares 172925.05=191447.61

For easy calculation, I ignore Brokerage on these examples.

On 16 Dec 11

Closed price 69.1

-17.01 % below from 200 DMA

(Actually, here Chandu need to sell 2 lot , one for 10% downside second for 15% downside but for easy calculation, here I give separate calculation, for each lot.)

So here first oldest buying lot was 177 shares Which he bought on 26 May 09.(Refer Balance sheet in excel sheet on 26 May 09 Chandu bought 177 shares @28.22 , Which we consider as the oldest lot.)

Chandu fill sell order for 177 Shares

Ordered Price=68.41 (last close 69.1-0.69) I think you remember when we put off-market sell order then always put price 1% below from closing price.

On next trading day, 19 Dec 11 Chandu order executed and Chandu sells his 177 Shares.

Total amount get=177 x68.41 =12108.57 Rupees

Principal Amount for these 177 Shares=177x28.22=4994.94 Rupees

Net Profit=12108.57-4994.94=7113.63 Rupees

Remain Shares = 2038

Market Value of Remain Shares=2038x68.41=139419.58

Remain Cash =3767.33+12108.57 =30631.13 Rupees

Net worth on 19 Dec 11 = Cash 30631.13+ Market value of remain 2038 shares 139419.58=170050.71

For easy calculation, I ignore Brokerage on these examples.

On 16 Dec 11

Closed price 69.1

-17.01 % below from 200 DMA

So here the second oldest buying lot was 156 Shares Which he bought on 28 May 09.(Refer Balance sheet in excel sheet on 28 May 09 Chandu bought 2 lot on the same day these 2 lots have 311 shares, so we decided 311/2=155.5 and rounded off it to 156.

These 156 shares @32.11 , Which we consider as the oldest lot.Remain 155 shares we consider in next selling)

Chandu fill sell order for 156 Shares

Ordered Price=68.41 (last close 69.1-0.69) I think you remember when we put off-market sell order then always put price 1% below from closing price.

On next trading day, 19 Dec 11 Chandu order executed and Chandu sells his 156 Shares.

Total amount get=156 x68.41 =10671.96 Rupees

Principal Amount for these 156 Shares=156x32.11=5009.16 Rupees

Net Profit=10671.96-5009.16=5662.8 Rupees

Remain Shares = 1882

Market Value of Remain Shares=1882x68.41=128747.62

Remain Cash =3767.33+10671.96 =41303.09 Rupees

Net worth on 19 Dec 11 = Cash 41303.09+ Market value of remain 1882 shares 128747.62=170050.71

For easy calculation, I ignore Brokerage on these examples.

On 28 Dec 11

Closed price 67.05

-21.52 % below from 200 DMA

Time to book profit in oldest buying.

So here oldest buying lot was 155 Shares Which he bought on 28 May 09.(Refer Balance sheet in excel sheet on 28 May 09 Chandu bought 155 shares @32.11 , Which we consider as the oldest lot.)

Chandu fill sell order for 155 Shares

Ordered Price=66.38 (last close 67.05-0.67) I think you remember when we put off-market sell order then always put price 1% below from closing price.

On next trading day, 29 Dec 11 Chandu order executed and Chandu sells his 155 Shares.

Total amount get=155 x66.38 =10288.9 Rupees

Principal Amount for these 155 Shares=155x32.11=4977.05 Rupees

Net Profit=10288.9-4977.05=5311.85 Rupees

Remain Shares = 1727

Market Value of Remain Shares=1727x66.38=114638.26

Remain Cash =3767.33+10288.9 =51591.99 Rupees

Net worth on 29 Dec 11 = Cash 51591.99+ Market value of remain 1727 shares 114638.26=166230.25

For easy calculation, I ignore Brokerage on these examples.

On 02 Jan 12

Closed price 64.95

-25.68 % below from 200 DMA

Time to book profit in oldest buying.

So here oldest buying lot was 145 Shares Which he bought on 1 June 09.(Refer Balance sheet in excel sheet on 1 June 09 Chandu bought 145 shares @34.54 , Which we consider as the oldest lot.)

Chandu fill sell order for 145 Shares

Ordered Price=64.31 (last close 64.95-0.64) I think you remember when we put off-market sell order then always put price 1% below from closing price.

On next trading day, 3 Jan 12 Chandu order executed and Chandu sells his 145 Shares.

Total amount get=145 x64.31 =9324.95 Rupees

Principal Amount for these 145 Shares=145x34.54=5008.3 Rupees

Net Profit=9324.95-5008.3=4316.65 Rupees

Remain Shares = 1582

Market Value of Remain Shares=1582x64.31=101738.42

Remain Cash =3767.33+9324.95 =60916.94 Rupees

Net worth on 3 Jan 12 = Cash 60916.94+ Market value of remain 1582 shares 101738.42=162655.36

For easy calculation, I ignore Brokerage on these examples.

20

How Chandu Deal With 2012 Volatility

I knew readers feel boring when they read calculations or data in this book.

And 2012 is the very volatile year for Arvind if I give all calculation, in this book then this book may bore you.

So in this chapter, I give only a very short brief of Chandu buying, selling, and profit booking during this volatility.

Why 2012 price is so volatile:-Market knew everything so whenever a big movement either downside or either upside will coming at any stock then price of that stock will more volatile than normal.

Arvind is now preparing for his big journey for demerger and higher valuation above 400.

So during this preparation, you see many time price of Arvind was fall below from 200 DMA and rise above 200 DMA because many investors who feel trap between 70 to 140 try to get an exit on every rise.

Arvind Stock rise again as below image:-

Chandu MS Excel Sheet of Sharegenius Software with Arvind Ltd

Date	Close Price	200 DMA	Change	% Variation
18-Jan-12	88.25	83.15	5.10	5.78
19-Jan-12	91	83.26	7.74	8.51
20-Jan-12	89.7	83.37	6.33	7.06
23-Jan-12	88.2	83.47	4.73	5.36
24-Jan-12	88.7	83.56	5.14	5.79
25-Jan-12	87.95	83.65	4.30	4.89
27-Jan-12	93.75	83.76	9.99	10.66
30-Jan-12	91.95	83.88	8.07	8.78
31-Jan-12	96.55	84.02	12.53	12.98
1-Feb-12	95.1	84.15	10.95	11.51
2-Feb-12	91.95	84.24	7.71	8.39
3-Feb-12	95.95	84.35	11.60	12.09
6-Feb-12	92.85	84.44	8.41	9.05
7-Feb-12	89.85	84.52	5.33	5.93
8-Feb-12	91.75	84.59	7.16	7.80
9-Feb-12	96.55	84.69	11.86	12.28
10-Feb-12	101.9	84.81	17.09	16.77

So here the summary of next 3 buying:-

On 18 Jan 12

Closed price 88.25

5.78% above from 200 DMA

Time to order for 5% fresh upside

Ordered 57 shares @89.13(88.25+0.88)

On next trading day, (19 Jan 12) Chandu order executed and Chandu bought 57 Shares.

Fresh investment=57 x 89.13=5080.41

Total shares on 19 Jan 12= 1639

Remain Cash = 60916.94-5080.41=55836.53

For easy calculation, I ignore Brokerage on these examples.

On 19 Jan 12

Chandu total Arvind shares= 1639

Market price per shares=89.13

Market value =1639x89.13= 146084.07

Net worth=Cash 55836.53+ Market value of Shares146084.07=201920.6

On 27 Jan 12

Closed price 93.75

10.66% above from 200 DMA

Time to order for 10% fresh upside

Ordered 53 shares @94.68(93.75+0.93)

On next trading day, (30 Jan 12) Chandu order executed and Chandu bought 53 Shares.

Fresh investment=53 x 94.68=5018.04

Total shares on 30 Jan 12= 1692

Remain Cash = 55836.53-5018.04=50818.49

For easy calculation, I ignore Brokerage on these examples.

On 30 Jan 12

Chandu total Arvind shares= 1692

Market price per shares=94.68

Market value =1692x94.68= 160198.56

Net worth=Cash 50818.49+ Market value of Shares160198.56=211017.05

On 10 Feb 12

Closed price 101.9

16.77% above from 200 DMA

Time to order for 15% fresh upside

Ordered 49 shares @102.91(101.9+1.01)

On next trading day, (13 Feb 12) Chandu order executed and Chandu bought 49 Shares.

Fresh investment=49 x 102.91=5042.59

Total shares on 13 Feb 12= 1741

Remain Cash = 50818.49-5042.59=45775.9

For easy calculation, I ignore Brokerage on these examples.

On 13 Feb 12

Chandu total Arvind shares= 1741

Market price per shares=102.91

Market value =1741x102.91= 179166.31

Net worth=Cash 45775.9+ Market value of Shares179166.31=224942.21

From 24 Feb 2012 Stock start falling again, but Chandu was happy in every condition because if the stock price rises he increase his holding and his net worth also rise.

If the stock price falls then, he decreases his holding and start profit booking in his earlier buying's and get tax-free profits in falling market.

Tax-free means when you sell a stock before 1 year then as per current Indian income tax law, you need to pay 15% flat short term capital gain tax on profits, but if you sell after 1 year, then your returns are tax-free.

Here system automatic suggest for selling, and Chandu sells oldest buying first so in every profit booking his shares are 2-3 years old when they trigger for a sellout.

So Chandu gets tax free profits when the market falls.

So here are the short briefs of next selling cycle:-

Date				
24-Feb-12	79.65	85.78	-6.13	-7.69
27-Feb-12	80.4	85.82	-5.42	-6.75
28-Feb-12	85	85.88	-0.88	-1.04
29-Feb-12	86.25	85.96	0.29	0.34
1-Mar-12	87.3	86.03	1.27	1.46
2-Mar-12	88.3	86.10	2.20	2.49
3-Mar-12	87.1	86.17	0.93	1.06
5-Mar-12	86.45	86.25	0.20	0.23
6-Mar-12	82.8	86.31	-3.51	-4.24
7-Mar-12	84.2	86.37	-2.17	-2.57
9-Mar-12	85.5	86.42	-0.92	-1.07
12-Mar-12	84.7	86.44	-1.74	-2.05
13-Mar-12	89.05	86.49	2.56	2.87
14-Mar-12	86.3	86.54	-0.24	-0.28
15-Mar-12	85.6	86.56	-0.96	-1.13
16-Mar-12	83	86.58	-3.58	-4.31
19-Mar-12	82.25	86.58	-4.33	-5.27

On 24 Feb 12

Closed price 79.65

-7.69 % below from 200 DMA

Time to book profit in oldest buying.

 So a here oldest buying lot was 127 Shares Which he bought on 18 Sept 09.(Refer Balance sheet in excel sheet on 18 Sept 09 Chandu bought 127 shares @39.54 , Which we consider as the oldest lot.)

Chandu fill sell order for 127 Shares

Ordered Price=78.86 (last close 79.65-0.79) I think you remember when we put off-market sell order then always put price 1% below from closing price.

On next trading day 27, Feb 12 Chandu order executed and Chandu sells his 127 Shares.

Total amount get=127 x78.86 =10015.22 Rupees

Principal Amount for these 127 Shares=127x39.54=5021.58 Rupees

Net Profit=10015.22-5021.58=4993.64 Rupees

Remain Shares = 1614

Market Value of Remain Shares=1614x78.86=127280.04

Remain Cash =3767.33+10015.22 =55791.12 Rupees

Net worth on 27 Feb 12 = Cash 55791.12+ Market value of remain 1614 shares 127280.04=183071.16

For easy calculation, I ignore Brokerage on these examples.

I hope you remember my earlier rule which I tell you in Chapter 6 of this book .If you forget it, then I repeat it here " ___Whenever your stock %___ ___variation from 200 DMA recover from (-) sign___ ___to (+) sign then every time you consider it as a___ ___starting point . it means if your stock recovers___ ___from -% variation below 200 DMA to +%___ ___variation above 200 DMA then you bought your___ ___one lot (start investing with one part of your___ ___money)."___

Opposite of this rule is also applicable when we sell out stocks, here is the opposite of this rule;-

" ___Whenever your stock % variation from 200___ ___DMA down again from (+) sign to (-) sign then___ ___every time you consider it as a fresh selling___ ___point . it means if your stock down from +%___ ___variation above 200 DMA to -5% variation___ ___below 200 DMA then you sell your one lot (start___ ___selling with your oldest buying)."___

For example on 24 Feb 2012 stock down -7.69% below from 200 DMA, so Chandu sell one oldest buying for 5% downside, and next selling will trigger when stock down 10% or more but on 29 Feb 12 stock again close 0.34% above from his 200 DMA so stock enter in +% zone.

So when stock again falls Chandu again sell oldest buying for -5%,-10%,-15%,-20%...every five multiple downsides.

Same happen between 19 Mar 2012 and 26 Mar 12 where stock recover above 200 DMA but down again, So, on 26 Mar 2012 Chandu again start selling from -5% or more point.

If you feel difficulty to understand this mean you do not read this book page by page by starting point, so this is an easy formula of safe trading, but it requires reading my examples point by point. (Every Skip page you will lose your chance to understand the method)

See these examples and refer excel sheet you automatic understand

On 19 Mar 12

Closed price 82.25

-5.27 % below from 200 DMA

Time to book profit in oldest buying.

 So here oldest buying lot was 139 shares Which he bought on 22 Mar 10.(Refer Balance sheet in excel sheet on 22 Mar 10 Chandu bought 139 shares @36.05 , Which we consider as the oldest lot.)

Chandu fill sell order for 139 shares

Ordered Price=81.43 (last close 82.25-0.82) I think you remember when we put off-market sell order then always put price 1% below from closing price.

On next trading day, 20 Mar 12 Chandu order executed and Chandu sells his 139 Shares.

Total amount get=139 x81.43 =11318.77 Rupees

Principal Amount for these 139 Shares=139x36.05=5010.95 Rupees

Net Profit=11318.77-5010.95=6307.82 Rupees

Remain Shares = 1475

Market Value of Remain Shares=1475x81.43=120109.25

Remain Cash =3767.33+11318.77 =67109.89 Rupees

Net worth on 20 Mar 12 = Cash 67109.89+ Market value of remain 1475 shares 120109.25=187219.14

For easy calculation, I ignore Brokerage on these examples.

between 19 Mar 2012 and 26 Mar 12 where stock recover above 200 DMA but down again, On 26 Mar 2012 Chandu again start selling from -5% or more point.

On 26 Mar 12

Closed price 81.7

-5.95 % below from 200 DMA

Time to book profit in oldest buying.

So here oldest buying lot was 138 Shares Which he bought on 22 Apr 10.(Refer Balance sheet in excel sheet on 22 Apr 10 Chandu bought 138 shares @36.36 , Which we consider as the oldest lot.)

Chandu fill sell order for 138 Shares

Ordered Price=80.89 (last close 81.7-0.81) I think you remember when we put off-market sell order then always put price 1% below from closing price.

On next trading day, 27 Mar 12 Chandu order executed and Chandu sells his 138 Shares.

Total amount get=138 x80.89 =11162.82 Rupees

Principle Amount for these 138 Shares=138x36.36=5017.68 Rupees

Net Profit=11162.82-5017.68=6145.14 Rupees

Remain Shares = 1337

Market Value of Remain Shares=1337x80.89=108149.93

Remain Cash =3767.33+11162.82 =78272.71 Rupees

Net worth on 27 Mar 12 = Cash 78272.71+ Market value of remain 1337 shares 108149.93=186422.64

For easy calculation, I ignore Brokerage on these examples.

On 9 May 12

Closed price 77.1

-12.72 % below from 200 DMA

Time to book profit in oldest buying.

So here oldest buying lot was 260 shares Which he bought on 6 Aug 10 11 Aug 10.(Refer

Balance sheet in excel sheet on 6 Aug 10 11 Aug 10 Chandu bought 260 shares @37.52 , Which we consider as the oldest lot.)

Chandu fill sell order for 260 shares

Ordered Price=76.33 (last close 77.1-0.77) I think you remember when we put off-market sell order then always put price 1% below from closing price.

On next trading day, 10 May 12 Chandu order executed and Chandu sells his 260 shares.

Total amount get=260 x76.33 =19845.8 Rupees

Principle Amount for these 260 Shares=260x37.52=9755.2 Rupees

Net Profit=19845.8-9755.2=10090.6 Rupees

Remain Shares = 1077

Market Value of Remain Shares=1077x76.33=82207.41

Remain Cash =3767.33+19845.8 =98118.51 Rupees

Net worth on 10 May 12 = Cash 98118.51+
Market value of remain 1077 shares
82207.41=180325.92

For easy calculation, I ignore Brokerage on these
examples.

On 14 May 12

Closed price 74.15

-17 % below from 200 DMA

Time to book profit in oldest buying.

 So here oldest buying lot was 115 shares Which
he bought on 18 Aug 10.(Refer Balance sheet in
excel sheet on 18 Aug 10 Chandu bought 115
shares @39.79 , Which we consider as the oldest
lot.)

Chandu fill sell order for 115 shares

Ordered Price=73.41 (last close 74.15-0.74) I
think you remember when we put off-market sell
order then always put price 1% below from
closing price.

On next trading day, 15 May 12 Chandu order
executed and Chandu sells his 115 shares.

Total amount get=115 x73.41 =8442.15 Rupees

Principle Amount for these 115 Shares=115x39.79=4575.85 Rupees

Net Profit=8442.15-4575.85=3866.3 Rupees

Remain Shares = 962

Market Value of Remain Shares=962x73.41=70620.42

Remain Cash =3767.33+8442.15 =106560.66 Rupees

Net worth on 15 May 12 = Cash 106560.66+ Market value of remain 962 shares 70620.42=177181.08

For easy calculation, I ignore Brokerage on these examples.

On 17 May 12

Closed price 70.7

-22.41 % below from 200 DMA

Time to book profit in oldest buying.

 So here oldest buying lot was 110 Shares Which he bought on 8 Sep 10.(Refer Balance sheet in excel sheet on 8 Sep 10 Chandu bought 110 shares @43.53 , Which we consider as the oldest lot.)

Chandu fill sell order for 110 shares

Ordered Price=70 (last close 70.7-0.7), I think you remember when we put off-market sell order then always put price 1% below from closing price.

On next trading day, 18 May 12 Chandu order executed and Chandu sells his 110 Shares.

Total amount get=110 x70 =7700 Rupees

Principal Amount for these 110 Shares=110x43.53=4788.3 Rupees

Net Profit=7700-4788.3=2911.7 Rupees

Remain Shares = 852

Market Value of Remain Shares=852x70=59640

Remain Cash =3767.33+7700 =114260.66 Rupees

Net worth on 18 May 12 = Cash 114260.66+ Market value of remain 852 shares 59640=173900.66

For easy calculation, I ignore Brokerage on these examples.

On 19 June 12

Closed price 68.65

-25.6 % below from 200 DMA

Time to book profit in oldest buying.

So here oldest buying lot was 97 Shares Which he bought on 14 Oct 10.(Refer Balance sheet in excel sheet on 14 Oct 10 Chandu bought 97 shares @51.76 , Which we consider as the oldest lot.)

Chandu fill sell order for 97 Shares

Ordered Price=67.97 (last close 68.65-0.68) I think you remember when we put off-market sell order then always put price 1% below from closing price.

On next trading day, 20 June 12 Chandu order executed and Chandu sells his 97 Shares.

Total amount get=97 x67.97 =6593.09 Rupees

Principal Amount for these 97 Shares=97x51.76=5020.72 Rupees

Net Profit=6593.09-5020.72=1572.37 Rupees

Remain Shares = 755

Market Value of Remain Shares=755x67.97=51317.35

Remain Cash =3767.33+6593.09 =120853.75 Rupees

Net worth on 20 June 12 = Cash 120853.75+ Market value of remain 755 shares 51317.35=172171.1

For easy calculation, I ignore Brokerage on these examples.

On 29 Aug 12

Closed price 60.75

-31.35 % below from 200 DMA

Time to book profit in oldest buying.

So here oldest buying lot was 89 Shares Which he bought on 20 Oct 10.(Refer Balance sheet in excel sheet on 20 Oct 10 Chandu bought 89 shares @56.56 , Which we consider as the oldest lot.)

Chandu fill sell order for 89 shares

Ordered Price=60.15 (last close 60.75-0.6) I think you remember when we put off-market sell order then always put price 1% below from closing price.

On next trading day, 30 Aug 12 Chandu order executed and Chandu sells his 89 Shares.

Total amount get=89 x60.15 =5353.35 Rupees

Principal Amount for these 89 Shares=89x56.56=5033.84 Rupees

Net Profit=5353.35-5033.84=319.51 Rupees

Remain Shares = 666

Market Value of Remain Shares=666x60.15=40059.9

Remain Cash =3767.33+5353.35 =126207.1 Rupees

Net worth on 30 Aug 12 = Cash 126207.1+ Market value of remain 666 shares 40059.9=166267

For easy calculation, I ignore Brokerage on these examples.

In next Chapter, we learn about Chandu dividend gain and saving account interest gain on his cash.

21

Chandu First Dividend Gain

Arvind Ltd declares 1 rupee per share dividend on 13 Sept 2012. Chandu holds 666 shares on 13 Sept 2012, so he gets INR 666 as his first dividend income.

After this dividend, Chandu net Cash holding was INR 126873.10.

So Chandu Cost of holding for 666 Arvind share was Zero because he starts his investment from INR 1,00,000 and due to his profit booking of INR 68347.40 and Saving Ac interest on cash holding , he has 666 shares and 126873.10 rupees cash.

Date	Buy	Price @	Total Inestment	Saving Ac Interest	Dividend gain	Cash in hand
13-Sep-12	-	-	-	-	666	126873.1
19-Sep-12	-	-	-	2270.56	-	129143.66

If Chinki still holds his initial 710 shares then on 13 Sept 2012 price of Arvind Ltd was 70.10 only, and she may be still in a loss of INR 50000 if she still holds her shares.

Ok, on the 7th anniversary of Chandu and Chinki initial investment, Chandu get INR 2270.56 as 4% saving account interest on his cash holding.

So now Chandu total cash is 129143.66, and Chandu still waits when his sharegenius software triggers next buying or selling in Arvind Ltd.

Now you completely learn my method so I cannot give a short brief of each buying and selling on this book.

Refer your excel sheet which you download from my google drive, In this sheet, I give Chandu complete balance sheet and buying and selling details so for detail of further buying and selling direct refer this excel sheet till 26.03.2013 where Chandu book some short loss due to selling trigger in software.

But as I tell earlier that these short losses are not a loss because they increase Chandu cash amount and Chandu get saving account interest on his cash, and due to this huge cash Chandu get INR 4520 as 4% saving account interest, so this short loss is easily recovered by interest.

Why software trigger for sell where upside in stock remain:- I invent this formula not only for Arvind Ltd, this formula work for all good volume stocks in the stock market.

If Arvind price does not rise from here, then this profit booking is protected you from loss and secure your earlier profits.

One more interesting thing you may note on your sheet that on 26 Mar 13, 1 Apr 13, 25 Apr 13 Chandu book loss but his net worth is increased.

Two Reasons of Increasing Net Worth:-

Because of remaining share, It is sufficient to increase your net worth if the stock rises again. The second reason we consider oldest buying lot price for calculating profit and loss, but if we consider Average Buying Price for calculating profit or loss, then you see this 2013 loss booking is actually a profit booking.

22

Demerger Of Arvind Ltd

Refer your excel sheet which you download from my google drive, In this sheet I give Chandu complete balance sheet and buying and selling details so for detail of further buying and selling direct refer this excel sheet till 28.05.2015, because on 28.05.15 Arvind Ltd demerger into two separate companies one is Arvind Ltd second Arvind Infrastructure Ltd (Currently known as Arvind Smartspaces Ltd).

So Chandu gets 44 Arvind Infra share because on 28 May 2015 Chandu hold 440 Arvind Ltd shares and as per swap ratio of 10:1 Chandu get 44 shares.

Which he sell on 12 Feb 16 at price of 77.1 because of that time Arvind stock trigger again for selling.

Arvind Ltd and Arvind infra have co shareholding in each other so when this downfall start Chandu also sell Arvind Infra 44 share @77.10 on 12 Feb closing price

This is the another example of my honesty because Arvind Infra touches an all-time high of 118 on 15 Jan 16 but I do not show Chandu sell his stocks @118 because it is unlogical to sell without any trigger.

23

How To Increase Your Investment

When your cash holding is increased more than your basic amount then increase your lot size as per this rule:-

Basic lot size=5000 rupees

Basic investment=1,00,000 rupees

If your cash increase between 1,00,000 to 2,00,000 then double your basic lot size means you invest 10,000 at a time if you have more than 1 lac in cash

Increase further size if your cash is between 2,00,000 to 3,00,000 then you invest 15000 at a time.

Means when your cash increase from your basic investment amount than doubles your partial investment amount.

If basic investment amount increases more then double then increase your partial investment amount triple for example:-

Start with 1 lac cash

Below 1 lac cash invest 5000 at a time.

Between 1 lac to 2 lac invest 10000 at a time.

Between 2 lac to 3 lac invest 15000 at a time.

Between 3 lac to 4 lac invest 20000 at a time.

Because as your cash increased your risk taking capacity also increased.

Refer Chandu 8 July 15 buying where his net cash 240440.80 so he invests INR 15000 on 8 July.

24

Happy Ending Of Story

Refer the last page of your Excel sheet on 15 Nov 16 Chandu has net cash of 154851.40, and he holds 558 Arvind shares as per my system.

The market value of these 558 shares was INR187156, and net worth of Chandu was INR 342007.40 .

Some of the readers have a question that if Chinki still holds her 710 shares, then she may win here or not?

It is very hard to hold a stock for an 11-year long time when you see downfall from 140 to 12 only.

But if Chinki still holds like Warren Buffett then here is her estimated balance sheet:-

If Chinki still hold his 710 shares then market value						233945
Market value of Arvind Smart space						6840.85
				dividend	1.65	1171.5
				dividend	2.35	1668.5
				dividend	2.55	1810.5
				dividend	2.4	1704
	interest on dividend cash					600.66
						247741

If Chinki still holds her 710 shares, then her net worth may be INR 247741 including all dividends, demerger, and interest but Chandu net worth is 342007.40.

So Chandu earns 242007.40 in this type of stock which not perform between 2005 to 2011.

Now Chandu sells all of his stocks and gets INR 342007; He gives INR 242000 to his best friend Chinki who lost her money in stock market.

Chandu gives 242000 to Chinki because if Chinki was not seen this dream then he unable to learn this trading system.

However, Chinki is the fiancée of Chandu.

Now Chandu starts this system again with his remain 1 lac in Country Club Hospitality and Holidays Ltd stock.

Chinki also starts this system in Vijaya Bank Stock.

They both come to me and tell their story to me, So I write this book for you.

I also advised them that instead of holding their money in saving account they hold 20,000 in cash and remaining 80000 may invest it in HDFC Top 200 Growth fund and as they utilized their fund and selling will not trigger then refill cash from the selling of mutual fund units.

In this method, they always fully invested in the market and get more than saving account interest for their cash holding.

Read more details about how to get tax free cash from mutual funds at this link:-

http://mutualfundgenius.maheshkaushik.co
m/2016/03/equity-mutual-funds-that-pay-
monthly.html

Discloser:- I am also holding Country Club
shares with the help of this system and my
wife (Mrs.Seema Kaushik, not Chinki) also
holding Vijaya Bank shares with the help
of this system.

25

FAQ

I add this chapter in 2nd Edition of my book because some of my followers ask questions when they read the first edition of this book so here is these question and their answers:-

1. Question 1:-In chapter 11 of your book you write that "If you agree to spend 5 minutes per day for your excel software, then this book lighting up your mind and no one stops you from becoming a millionaire in coming 10 years" Why you use millionaire word in this chapter? I read the whole book and find Chandu start his investment with 1,00,000 rupees and earn only 242007.40 rupees, So why you use word "millionaire"?

2. Answer 1:- Thank you for your query, In my example Chandu hold cash in his saving account, If you read complete book

then in last page you knew I suggest to invest 80% cash in Mutual fund units and hold remaining 20% in cash, as you utilized cash refill them by selling of mutual fund unit it will increase your 4% return on saving account cash to 12% return.

Second thing , I am the honest person and choose Arvind stock in my book which down from 140 to 12 then rise from 12 to 400. Arvind stock does not perform well during 2005 to 2014 and does not recover his price 140 again during 2005 to 2014.

So during these first 9 years of 2005 to 2014 people recover his initial money but Chandu makes profits in this worst period.

If you apply this formula on 5 other continues performing stocks with mutual fund cash parking; then you wonder to see results.

For example download, last 10-year price history of Cera Sanitary, Butterfly

Gandhimati Appliances, Bata India, Amara Raja Batteries, Goodyear India, Sun pharma, etc., Start with 5 lac cash, and run my formula in any 5 stocks of above 6 stocks with mutual fund cash parking you will touch a million figure.

Question 2:- If I want to start your method in 3 Stocks then I need 3,00,000 rupees, but I have only 2,00,000 rupees. What to do?

Answer 2:- All stocks not up and down at once so with 2 lac cash you reserve 20% of your money for cash holding.

It means hold 40,000 in cash and invest remaining 160000 in any good equity mutual fund now invest INR 5000-5000-5000 in your 3 stocks and if formula suggests further buy then use remaining cash and do not forget to refill your cash by selling of mutual fund units.

If you sell stocks and get cash then invest additional cash in mutual fund again.

Question 3:-I am a trader and do not want to invest for such a long period of 10 years so how I use your system in my short term trading?

Answer 3:-Read next chapter of this book where you find how to use my innovation in regular trading.

26

How To Use This System In Regular Trading?

Before I complete this book, I want to highlight your attention on a quote from Steve Jobs (Co-founder, chairman, and chief executive officer of Apple Inc.).

In Steve Jobs words "When you grow up, you tend to get told the world is the way it is and your life is just to live your life inside the world. Try not to bash into the walls too much. Try to have a nice family, have fun, save a little money. That's a very limited life.

Life can be much broader once you discover one simple fact:- **Everything around you that you call life was made up by people that were no smarter than you and you can change it, you can influence it, you can build your own things that other people can use.**

Once you learn that, you'll never be the same again."

It means I want to say that I am not more smart than you because **only smartest people who really want to learn that how to earn money from stock market will reach on this page, other quickly read few of starting page and then stop reading**.

So If you really complete the whole book and reach on these last pages then you are among the smartest people and as Steve Jobs say **"Everything around you that you call life was made up by people that were no smarter than you, and you can change it, you can influence it, you can build your own things that other people can use."**

Means you can now change my system as your requirement.

For example, If you want to use this system in your day to day stock market trading then this system is a gold mine for you.

How to use this system for trading ?

In Arvind Ltd example you find that *Arvind Ltd rise and up many time and most of the time when It rises from his 200 DMA, then maximum rising is capped at 35% or 40% or 45% of 200 DMA and stock never rise more than 50% from 200 DMA in last 10 year.*

Arvind price rises from 12 to 400, but the stock does not rise more than 50% from 200 DMA in last 10 year.

Why?

I have an answer:-

Most of the stock does not rise more than 50% above from 200 DMA because as stock price rise, 200 DMA also rise day by day and as stock price fall, 200 DMA also fall day by day.

So what happen if you invest a lump sum amount of INR 50,000 when stock rise 5% above from 200 DMA and book your partial profits after 15%,20%,25%, 30% and 35% rising from 200 DMA?

It means **whenever any stock rise from (-)% variation and close + 5% above from 200 DMA then invest a lump sum amount near INR 50,000 in that stock.**

Now divide your total holding into 5 parts and sell 1/5 part of your holding when stock rise more than 15% from 200 DMA.

Sell next 1/5 part when stock rise more than 20% from 200 DMA.

Sell next 1/5 when stock rise more than 25% from 200 DMA.

Sell next 1/5 part when stock rise more than 30% from 200 DMA.

Sell last 1/5 part when stock rise more than 35% from 200 DMA.

What to do if the stock starts downtrend again after 5% rising:-

Check this on your Arvind Ltd data sheet. Suppose on 22 March 2010 you invest INR 50000 lump sum amount in Arvind Ltd because on 19 March 2010 stock close 5.28% above from 200 DMA.

Suppose on 22 March 2010 you buy 1387 Arvind stocks @36.05

Unfortunately, stock down again after your buying, So in this situation what our stop loss is?

We also divide our stop loss into 5 parts.

It means we sell 1/5 part of our holding when stock close (-)5% below from 200 DMA, Sell next 1/5 part when stock close (-)10% below from 200 DMA.

So every 5% fall from 200 DMA means at levels of -5%, -10%, -15%, -20% and -25% we sell 1/5,1/5,1/5,1/5 and 1/5 parts of our holding.

So in this 2010 market fall, you sell 60% of your holding (3 parts of 1/5) and book loss (near 4000 rupees) on 7 May 2010, 21 May 2010 and 25 May 2010.

Now you hold your remain 40% share(556 shares) and cash (26057.40 rupees).

On 05 Aug 2010 stock again close above 5% from 200 DMA, so we reinvest this cash 26057.40 rupees here and buy 694 stock again.

Now our total stocks 556+694=1250 So in this downfall we lost only 137 stocks.

After that, you see that stock run till 40% above from 200 DMA and you sell 1/5 part of these 1250 shares at every 5% rise from 200 DMA.

It means we book partial profits at every 5% rise and sell our 250-250-250-250 and 250 shares at 15%,20%,25%,30%, and 35% rise from 200 DMA.

This will not only recover our loss of 4000 rupees but also give us a decent profit near 13000 rupees.

If you put this example on your whole sheet of Arvind Ltd, you wonder that you got decent profits many times.

27

Your Homework

When you learn in a school, your teacher gives you homework.

For learning a skill practice is a necessary requirement.

In this book, I tell you a skill that how you identify any stock entry and exit point for investment and trading purpose but for a complete understanding of this skill more practice is required from your side.

So here is your homework:-

Download last 3-year price data of any five stocks of your choice.

 Now apply Chapter 26 Concept on these 5 shares.

It means notionally invest a lump-sum notional amount INR 50,000 when stock rise from (-)% to +5% .

And start selling after 15% rise , sell 20% of stocks when the stock rises +15% from 200 DMA, sell next 20% stocks when stock rise +20% from 200 DMA.

It means book your partial profits after 15%, 20%,25%, 30% and 35% rising from 200 DMA and as stop loss sell 1/5 part or 20% of your holding at every -5%,-10%-15%,-20% and -25% fall from 200 DMA.

What do you find from this exercise?

Do not e-mail your results to me, because I have more than 15000 followers, so I am unable to check your sheets and unable to reply all e-mails.

So share short brief of your results in your review on Amazon site.

What do you learn from this book?

What do you find in your homework?

Will you apply this system to your investment and trading strategy?

I wait for your reviews on Amazon site.

If you like this story, then please do not forget to review my book on Amazon site because your review gives me energy for my work.

Best of luck, Now I am waiting for your reviews.

DISCLAIMER

The author is NISM certified research analyst and registered with SEBI as a research analyst.

His comments are an expression of opinion only and should not be construed in any manner whatsoever as recommendations to buy or sell a stock, option, future, bond, commodity, index or any other financial instrument at any time. While he believes his statements to be true, they always depend on the reliability of his own credible sources.

All company names (Arvind Ltd, Country Club Hospitality and Holidays Ltd, Vijaya Bank, etc.) are trademarks™ or registered® trademarks of their respective holders. Use of them does not imply any affiliation with or endorsement by them.

Subject to Pindwara (India) jurisdiction only.